Essentials of Organisational Behaviour in Africa

T0332552

A concise textbook focusing on organisational behaviour in the African context, this book is featured in Routledge's new *Essentials of Business and Management in Africa* shortform textbook series.

This book covers organisational behaviour concepts applicable to the African continent and its varied cultures. The chapters thoroughly explore topics including personal and individual factors, motivation, decision-making and communication, groups and teams, leadership and influence, conflict and negotiation. Each chapter refers to aspects of the African context such as cultural values, *Ubuntu*, and the informal economy and relates these to the topics discussed. The book includes illustrative real-life examples, vignettes, mini-cases and exercises. Undergraduate and postgraduate students in Africa, and with an interest in the area, will appreciate the focus on a region so little discussed in the business and management literature.

Filling a gap in the literature and including a dearth of material, this book will also appeal to current and future practicing managers in African countries, as well as those employed in government and by Non Governmental Organisations (NGOs).

Betty Jane Punnett is Professor Emerita at the University of the West Indies (Cave Hill), Barbados.

Thomas Anyanje Senaji is Associate Professor and Deputy Vice Chancellor at the East African University, Kenya.

Essentials of Business and Management in Africa
Series Editors: Bella Galperin, Terri Lituchy,
Betty Jane Punnett and Ali Taleb

This series of shortform textbooks offers a range of books which focus on the essentials of various aspects of business and management in the African context.

In focusing on the core elements of each sub-discipline, the books provide a useful alternative or supplement to traditional textbooks, and can be used by trainers and managers as well. Each book provides information on basic concepts in the sub-discipline and examples to illustrate how these concepts are affected by the African context.

Essentials of General Management in Africa
Lemayon Lemilia Melyoki and Betty Jane Punnett

Essentials of Organisational Behaviour in Africa
Betty Jane Punnett and Thomas Anyanje Senaji

For more information about this series, please visit: www.routledge. com/Essentials-of-Business-and-Management-in-Africa/book-series/ EBMA

Essentials of Organisational Behaviour in Africa

**Betty Jane Punnett and
Thomas Anyanje Senaji**

 Routledge
Taylor & Francis Group

NEW YORK AND LONDON

First published 2022
by Routledge
605 Third Avenue, New York, NY 10158

and by Routledge
4 Park Square, Milton Park, Abingdon, Oxon, OX14 4RN

Routledge is an imprint of the Taylor & Francis Group, an informa business

Library of Congress Cataloging-in-Publication Data
Names: Punnett, Betty Jane, author. | Anyanje Senaji, Thomas, author.
Title: Essentials of organisational behaviour in Africa / Betty Jane Punnett and Thomas Anyanje Senaji.
Description: 1 Edition. | New York, NY : Routledge, 2022. | Series: Essentials of business and management in Africa | Includes bibliographical references and index.
Identifiers: LCCN 2021059470 | ISBN 9780367478445 (hardback) | ISBN 9780367435219 (paperback) | ISBN 9781003036838 (ebook)
Subjects: LCSH: Organizational change—Africa. | Teams in the workplace—Africa. | Management—Africa. | Decision making—Africa.
Classification: LCC HD58.7 .P856 2022 | DDC 658.0096—dc23/eng/20211207
LC record available at https://lccn.loc.gov/2021059470

ISBN: 978-0-367-47844-5 (hbk)
ISBN: 978-0-367-43521-9 (pbk)
ISBN: 978-1-003-03683-8 (ebk)

DOI: 10.4324/9781003036838

Typeset in Times New Roman
by KnowledgeWorks Global Ltd.

For our granddaughter and son, Luzviminda and Nathan, who keep the house warm with their presence, and Jacqueline Rose Anyango for invaluable support. May Nightingale Khamonya, Victor, Franklin and George be inspired by this work.

For our granddaughter Jessica who loved Africa when the lions roared for her birthday.

Contents

Figures and table

Figures

Table

1 Introduction to Organisational Behaviour

Learning Outcomes

After completing this chapter, you will be able to:

- Define organisations
- Describe organisational behaviour
- Explain the meaning and impact of culture in organisations
- Explain additional aspects of context that relate to culture
- Examine organisational behaviour in the African context

Thought Starters

Proverb – a simple, traditional saying expressing a perceived truth based on common sense or experience. Proverbs are often metaphorical and need to be interpreted. Some African examples:

> *Ingoi yivula lisimba,* translated as "a leopard begets a mongoose" – Tiriki, Kenya
> *The monkey requested for a long tail and it was given* – Luo, Kenya
> *When the shepherd comes home in peace, the milk is sweet* – Ethiopia
> *The enemy does not fall where you throw it* – Kikuyu, Kenya
> *When you befriend a chief, remember that he sits on a rope* – Uganda
> *The night has ears* – Maasai, Kenya

Summary

This chapter summarises what we mean by organisations and organisational behaviour (OB), and why understanding behaviour is critical to effective management and organisational performance/success. It considers the African context and relates this to behaviour. We discuss culture, present models of culture and available scores for

DOI: 10.4324/9781003036838-1

African countries. The chapter briefly considers politics and economics, history and geography, language and religion, as they relate to OB.

Introduction

Recently, Africa has been seen as an attractive place to do business. African Economic Outlook (2019) shows real GDP growth was 2.1% in 2016, 3.6% in 2017, 3.5% in 2018 and projected at 4% and 4.1% for 2019 and 2020, higher than many other emerging/developing economies (lower than China and India, but China and India are countries while Africa is a continent with many diverse countries). The actual 2020 growth may be lower because of COVID-19 but forecasts remain optimistic. Inward and outward foreign direct investment has increased substantially and economic prospects have generally been positive. The uncertain global economy, political challenges, instability and poverty remain real for many African countries and dealing with these is a priority. This context needs to be understood to manage effectively in Africa.

Doing business in Africa requires recognition of diversity – across countries and within a country. Jackson (2004) argued that African managers deal effectively with multiple stakeholders and focus attention on people in their own right. Amoako-Agyei (2009) cautions that successful globalisation into Africa requires managers to have in-depth understanding of African cultural values and their impact on behaviour. Most African countries are collective and decisions are informed by community good, with individual gratification subservient to community wellbeing.

Organisations range from large, legal, registered enterprises (e.g., multinational corporations) to small 'mom and pop' shops. Organisations can be public, private, government, non-government, non-profit, local, national or international. We focus on business organisations, although OB concepts apply to all types of organisations. Managing a business includes coordinating resources (human, physical, financial) to achieve goals and provide profits. OB focuses on human resources, that is, people and is based on psychology, sociology, anthropology and economics. It asks why individuals/groups behave the way they do in organisations and seeks to understand and improve attitudes and behaviours and explain outcomes such as job performance and commitment. It sounds simple – to understand behaviour in organisations – but it is complex, because there are many factors which influence behaviour. OB can be defined as the study of human behaviour in organisational settings.

Early OB focused on productivity/performance and pay. Today OB is more complex and multi-faceted. In the late 1900s and early twentieth century, the belief was that people worked for economic reasons, efficiency resulted in increased performance and payment for performance was effective. This was known as scientific management and based on people behaving logically and rationally, essentially without emotions. Over time, behavioural scientists considered the human elements of work and people's emotions. They argued that people wanted to work for a variety of reasons, not just economic, and understanding emotions, needs, desires and so on, at work would contribute to performance/productivity. Next, the focus was the context of behaviour, and the impact of both the task and people dimensions of performance. Contingency theories integrated several considerations into understanding OB and these are relatively complex because they incorporate multiple perspectives. These will be explored in more detail in later chapters. OB is a growing field and becoming more important in the global economy where people of diverse backgrounds/values work together. It has been criticised for Western assumptions and scholars are seeking to expand its scope to include non-Western thinking. The world of work is also changing in the twenty-first century – more contract work, virtual work, networks and so on, some of which are being encouraged by the COVID-19 pandemic. These trends will impact behaviour at work, and we expect theories to expand and change to encompass shifts in the workplace.

It is important to understand the context within which behaviour takes place. Punnett (2019) identifies the following factors as relevant contextual factors.

Societal/National Culture

This focuses on 'the way of life of a group of people'. The group might be a society, nation state, region, ethnic group/tribe, etc. Culture is shared by group members, it is passed on by family and can be learned at homes, schools and religious/other organisations. Culture shapes values, attitudes, beliefs and behaviours, and cultures vary because of these.

Some cultural cues are easily identified – clothes, food, spoken language, music, movies, television shows, etc., are relatively obvious aspects of culture. Some groups use chopsticks, some knives/forks, some eat *ugali* or *fufu* with their fingers and Italians use a fork and spoon for spaghetti. One metaphor relates culture to an iceberg. An iceberg has visible parts on the surface of the water and invisible

Figure 1.1 Culture as an Iceberg.

Visible – e.g., Art, Dress, Food, Greetings, Language, and Literature.
Invisible – Assumptions, Beliefs, Biases, Norms and Values.

parts underwater; up to 90% of an iceberg's area can be hidden (see Figure 1.1). Similarly, culture and behaviours have both visible and invisible components, and it is easier to see and understand the visible aspects, above water, than those not visible, below water. Another metaphor is an island. Things on the surface of the island, mountains, valleys, rivers, forests, buildings can be seen, studied and understood – these are the equivalent of food, clothing, etc., but we cannot see what is below the surface. Values, attitudes and beliefs are aspects of culture which cannot be readily seen but must be discerned through experience.

Several cultural models have attempted to measure these aspects of culture by identifying cultural value dimensions.

Cultural Models

The best-known model, Hofstede's (1980, 2001) identifies:

> *Individualism/Collectivism* (IDV) – the extent to which people feel independent, versus being interdependent on members of a group.
> *Uncertainty Avoidance* (UAI) – the extent to which people tolerate uncertainty and ambiguity, versus anxiety and distrust of the unknown and preference for laws, rules, procedures, habits and rituals.
> *Masculinity/femininity* (MAS) – the extent to which assertiveness and competitiveness are accepted, and men are tough and 'bread winners', versus a focus on the quality of life and more sympathy and empathy for the unfortunate in society.
> *Power Distance* (PDI) – the extent to which people accept that power will be distributed unequally, versus equality being valued with few differences in power between members.
> *Long-term/orientation* (LTO) – the degree of concern and planning for the future, versus a focus on the immediate and short-term.
> *Indulgence/restraint* (IND) – the degree to which people do what they want to feel good and free, versus a belief that restraint is necessary, life is hard and duty is expected.

Hofstede's website provides maps and scores for countries around the world.

Noorderhaven and Tidjani (2001) identified a value dimension in African countries (Cameroon, Ghana, Senegal, South Africa, Tanzania, Zimbabwe) related to Hofstede's work. They found that 'traditional wisdom' was correlated with the Far East dimension of long-term orientation but had the following implications in the African context – *wisdom is more important than knowledge* and *wisdom comes from experience and time, not from education*. This seems to underscore African veneration for age and the wisdom age implies, but suggests a downplaying of the value of education.

Studies including African countries suggest that Kenya, Ethiopia, Tanzania and Zambia are short-term oriented (LTO = 25), collectivist

(IDV = 27) and moderate on power distance (PDI = 64). West African countries, Nigeria, Ghana, Sierra Leone (PDI = 77) and Egypt (PDI = 80) are higher on power distance. More generally, African countries are on the collective side of the scale, with a short-term orientation. Management should consider these cultural values relative to strategies, goals, structures, policies and procedures so they fit with the cultural context. For example, high power distance relates to acceptance of hierarchy, and short-term orientation relates to time frames for planning.

The Globe Project (House, 2004) looked at eight dimensions of culture, similar to Hofstede's:

Institutional Collectivism – degree to which society practices, encourages and rewards collective distribution of resources and collective action.

In-Group Collectivism – degree to which society expresses pride, loyalty and cohesiveness in groups (society, organisations, families, etc.).

Gender Egalitarianism – degree to which society promotes gender equality and minimises inequality.

Future Orientation – degree to which society engages in future-oriented behaviours such as planning/investing in the future.

Power Distance – degree to which society accepts and endorses authority, power differences and status privileges.

Uncertainty Avoidance – degree to which society relies on social norms, rules and procedures to alleviate unpredictability of future events.

Assertiveness – degree to which individuals are assertive, confrontational and aggressive in relationships with others.

Humane Orientation – degree to which society encourages and rewards fairness, altruism, generosity, caring and kindness.

Results for five Sub-Saharan African (SSA) countries, (Nigeria, Namibia, Zambia, Zimbabwe and South Africa – black sample) suggest common themes characterising SSA. One was *ubuntu*, reflecting high levels of group solidarity, and a paternalistic, humane-oriented leadership. Wanasika, Howell, Littrell, and Dorfman (2010) commented that "although the negative legacy of colonial dominance has contributed to a culture of corruption, poverty, tribalism and violence, charismatic leaders frequently invoke indigenous cultural values and means to overcome these problems" (p. 234).

Hofstede and GLOBE have a worldwide focus. The Leadership Effectiveness in Africa and the African Diaspora (LEAD) project focused on African countries. LEAD found five characteristics of an effective leader.

- A social leader – social, wise and hard working.
- A visionary servant leader – takes care of the community by participating in community projects and supporting followers.
- An inspirational leader – models good behaviours and inspires subordinates.
- A traditional leader – believes in following traditions and respecting gender roles.
- A delegative leader – believes in delegating authority to subordinates.

The LEAD findings corroborate Hofstede's, with respect and tradition important descriptors of culture in Africa (see Canadian Journal of Administrative Sciences, December 2014). African cultures have also been characterised by personal steadiness/stability, protecting 'face' and reciprocation of greetings/favours/gifts. Respect for tradition may inhibit implementation of change and possibly lead to a lack of innovation. Protecting 'face' may mean organisational members do not confront undesirable behaviours but cover them to avoid embarrassment. Reciprocity can result in ethical compromises (Tangpong, Li, Hung & Senaji, 2012).

There are many other models of culture and the reader should review these for additional insights on cultural values. See, for example, Schwartz (1992), Trompenaars and Hampden-Turner (1998) and World Values Survey (2018).

Ubuntu as an African world view and descriptor of African culture has received recent attention.

Ubuntu

Archbishop Desmond Tutu of South Africa said of *Ubuntu*:

A person is a person through other persons. None of us comes into the world fully formed. We would not know how to think, or walk, or speak, or behave as human beings unless we learned it from other human beings. We need other human beings in order to be human

(Tutu, 2004, p. 25).

The concept resonates with inclusivity. *Ubuntu* encompasses value systems, beliefs and practices common among African people (Mnyaka & Motlhabi, 2005), including core values of humaneness, caring, sharing, respect and compassion. Tutu says *Ubuntu* encompasses spiritual attributes including generosity, hospitality, compassion, caring and sharing; one can be rich in material possessions and lack *Ubuntu*. Ncube (2010) described *Ubuntu* as a set of institutionalised ideals, which guide and direct the patterns of life of Africans with its hallmark being concern with harmony, continuity and inclusivity. While this philosophy and African culture emphasise inclusiveness, the practice of leadership in government and organisations often appears quite different. Organisations need to consider how they can align practice with this philosophy.

Culture is influenced by other factors and influences those factors. Next, we outline some of these.

Politics and Economics

The world is largely made up of nation states, each with a government/political system. To do business within a state, or across national boundaries, companies must comply with national requirements, some relating to people and behaviour (including pay, benefits, working conditions, dress). Organisations need to be aware of national requirements and consider how they can be factored into operations to influence behaviour and accomplish desired objectives. For example, if a company provides bonuses to high performing employees and bonuses are limited by law, the company will want to consider different incentives, such as gifts, days off and the like; as well, individual and group bonuses should be sensitive to whether the society is *collectivist* or *individualist*.

The political system influences the type of management that is acceptable/typical in a country. Systems include dictatorships (some may be considered 'benign', seeking the good of the people), kingdoms (with a variety of succession possibilities and some 'constitutional', combined with forms of democracy), one party states (usually communist), two-party/multi-party and parliamentary democracies. The political system is often closely related to economic choices, with democracies favouring freer markets. This is not absolute, some kingdoms are free markets, and some democracies have substantial government control over business/organisations. There is likely a relationship between the government system and how management occurs; for example, more autocratic governments likely lead to more autocratic management.

Political systems vary widely across the African continent and this will influence how managers approach OB in different countries. The laws relating to behaviour need to be understood and the implications of the politics and how these are reflected in behaviour need to be considered in the design of organisations.

Some governments control the economy centrally and private enterprises are expected to work closely with the government. Where a country is governed by a 'strong man' or dictator, business decisions may need to conform to his (possibly her) preferences. If the leader decides that exploiting the rain forest will bring wealth to the regime, then businesses in the forestry harvesting sector will be encouraged. If the leader favours moving to alternative energy sources (e.g., solar, wind) these will be favoured.

Some political systems believe in free markets/capitalism and private enterprise is seen as the 'engine of growth'. Businesses have flexibility to carry out chosen strategies, with little interference from the government. Extremes of central control or total business freedom are not usual. Most countries have a mix of regulations to control certain types of organisations/activities, and some level of private enterprise. Some governments actively encourage investment, domestic and foreign, and provide incentives. Most governments have regulations to discourage or prohibit undesirable behaviours (slavery is outlawed by almost all governments and employees must be paid a 'fair' wage, often legally determined). The type of government, its decisions and its approach to business can have an important impact on economic development due to how it impacts economic socio-activity of organisations. In general, relatively free markets and democracies have been correlated with better development. In recent years, many African countries have made changes intended to make it easier to do business and investments have increased. African countries are also doing relatively well, economically, and this provides opportunities for businesses. These issues need to be considered in terms of management approaches and systems developed to encourage desired behaviour in organisations.

History and Geography

All countries are influenced by their history and history affects culture and behaviour. This is certainly true in Africa. The African continent is believed to be the birthplace of humans, the 'cradle of man', therefore, in some sense we are all part of the African diaspora. Historical events of the past 600 or so years have been described as having a major impact on the reality of Africa today. There are three main 'events' that influenced Africa over this period – the slave trade, colonialism and independence. Very briefly:

1 Although slave trading existed in Africa for a long time, the major impact came with the spread of the practice through the trans-Atlantic trade, where slaves were taken to the Americas, largely to work on plantations. According to Gilder Lehrman Institute of American History (accessed December 22, 2020), this trade lasted from approximately 1526 to 1867, and about 12.5 million slaves were shipped from Africa; 10.7 million to the Americas. The Atlantic Slave Trade was described as the costliest in human life of all long-distance global migrations. The impact on Africa was severalfold. Most obviously was the loss of human power and intellectual capital. In addition, Africans captured other Africans and sold them to the European slave traders. This occurred even at a local level causing hostile relations among different groups, which became one basis for what is sometimes now called 'tribal' differences. The slave trade engendered insecurity, violence and warfare with detrimental impacts on the institutional, social and economic development of African societies, including the deterioration of domestic legal institutions, the weakening of states and political and social fragmentation. Given the importance of institutions for economic development, the slave trade eroded the foundation on which African people could build their economies. When the slave trade was eventually abolished, it was replaced with colonialism.

2 Partitioning Africa by Europeans started in the 1860s and was completed by the early 1900s following the Berlin Conference of 1884 which formalised the 'Scramble for Africa'. By 1905, Western European governments claimed control of almost all of Africa. Britain and France had the largest holdings, but Germany, Spain, Italy, Belgium and Portugal had colonies. Africa lost sovereignty and control over its natural resources, and colonial powers signed treaties, and drew maps with boundaries for colonies, protectorates and 'free-trade' areas. Effects of the slave trade were reinforced, and civil conflict resulted when tribes/ethnic groups were divided into more than one country. Partition shaped the tribal/ethnic composition of states when they became independent, leading to ethnic polarisation, fractionalisation and inequality. This influenced institutional and economic development and provision of public goods and led to conflicts. Tribal/ethnic division is one

of the main legacies of colonialism which exacerbated the rivalries engendered by the slave trade. These factors contributed to in-group/out-group tendencies in workplaces, where managers may favour members of their own ethnic background. This can affect an organisation's ability to hire and develop staff, employees' motivation and commitment to the organisation, and foster allegiance to personal networks over the organisation.

3 By 1977, 54 African countries had become independent states. Colonisation resulted in a mix of states. Some are landlocked, inhibiting access to global markets, some tiny with few resources, others large with abundant resources. Some have peculiar shapes, limiting the reach of a state beyond its capital. These effects continue to impact the political, social, economic and cultural life of post-colonial Africa. In addition, former colonies may be controlled by colonisers through indirect means, such as foreign aid/loans, control of international financial institutions, interference in internal affairs and so on. After independence, African countries pursued strategies to bring about social and economic development, but problems related to weak economic growth began in the 1960s, and by the 1970s some countries had either stagnated or declined. The leaders of some newly independent countries continued colonial practices and treated their citizens like subjects and saw themselves as all-powerful rulers. This all meant that globally African countries were portrayed negatively, particularly in terms of doing business. This has been changing more recently, and several African countries are doing well, economically, politically and socially, with growth in trade, investment and Gross Domestic Product (GDP)/capita.

Africa is the second largest continent in the world (Asia, the largest), over 11.5 million square miles/30 million square kilometres, consisting of about 54 countries (sources give slightly different numbers) with a population of over a billion. It is divided into regions – north, south, west, east, central and sub-Saharan (countries south of the Saharan desert). There are economic groupings recognised by the Africa Union (AU) mirroring these.

African countries range from very large (Algeria – about 7% of the continent's land mass) to small island countries (the Seychelles, 115 islands along the eastern coast). Egypt belongs to the AU, although a small area is in Asia and it is often grouped with Middle East countries. The continent has many tribes/ethnic groups, with some very large and others small. The Democratic Republic of Congo, for example, has some 200 tribes/ethnic groups and Tanzania about 120.

The largest tribes/ethnic groups are the Fulani and Yoruba found in Nigeria. All tribes/ethnic groups have their own languages and cultures, for example, the Tiriki of Vihiga County of western Kenya occupy *iShamakho, iKaimosi, iSeremi* and *Cheptulu* areas, a few kilometres from Kisumu and Kakamega, and have a rich culture of rite of passage (*idumi*) for boys.

Language and Religion

Language and religion affect people's cultural beliefs and their behaviours. For example, language influences what people see. In the far north, where different kinds of snow are critical to survival, there are many more words for snow than elsewhere, and people see differences that are not apparent to others. Languages often have a hierarchy, some thought of as 'better' and spoken by the upper classes (upper class British spoke French and English words reflect this – e.g., 'chaise' considered upper class versus chair).

Religion is essentially about values which are reflected in behaviour. Religious beliefs state what is right/wrong and prescribe/proscribe behaviours. Certain religions prohibit eating certain foods (pork, beef, shellfish), some require/encourage fasting (Ramadan for Muslims, Lent for Christians), some keep men and women apart, some provide for mass weddings and so on. This means that it is important to understand the language(s) spoken in each location and to know the tenets of the different religion(s) that are practiced.

Africans were obliged to learn European languages, because Europeans considered colonisation a 'civilising mission' and had policies and cultural programs of 'assimilation'. Today this is reflected in the languages spoken in different countries – i.e., French in former French colonies, English in former British colonies, Portuguese in Mozambique and Angola. There are many native languages in Africa, and around a hundred are widely used for inter-ethnic communication, with Arabic, Somali, Berber, Amharic, Oromo, Igbo, Swahili, Hausa, Manding, Lingala, Fulani and Yoruba spoken by tens of millions of people. Expatriates spending any time in Africa will find it helpful to learn the local language, and when using a European language should keep in mind that this may in essence be a second language for others, even though they seem to speak fluently.

Religion in Africa is multi-faceted; Christianity is common throughout some countries, Islam in others and in still others, both are practiced (sometimes peacefully side by side, sometimes with antagonism between groups). There are several traditional animist religions and sometimes Christian/Islamic beliefs are combined with the beliefs/ practices of traditional religions. It was estimated in 2020 that about 40% of the overall population was Christian (Christians predominate in SSA) and 45% Islamic.

Context and Theory

Research on cultural differences has found that national culture affects the applicability of many theories, models and concepts. You cannot necessarily use a theory/model/concept developed in the West or China in Nigeria or Ethiopia. Punnett (2019) described Western OB theories as individualistic, based on a belief in equality, with a rational, linear logic. Africans tend to be more collective/communal, to see power differentials as acceptable, and to believe in the value of experience over logic. This will affect how OB theories are put into practice. For example, several theories of motivation (discussed in Chapter 4) focus on the individual, a desire for equity/equal treatment and the logical evaluation of various factors. In a communal society evaluation would be of the group rather than the individual, and outcomes or rewards would be for the community rather than the individual. Therefore, as we review theories/models/concepts, we should question if they apply in African countries, and how they need to be adapted to fit the context.

As more international organisations enter Africa, this context and how it influences OB is ever more relevant. Managers need to determine policies/practices to be adopted and adapted there. Expatriates living and working in African countries need to be trained, and as work groups become diverse, cultural differences must be considered. Some cultures appreciate monetary rewards more than other rewards, such as a commendation letter or being singled out as 'employee of the week'. It is important to differentiate rewards depending on cultural preferences.

In North America, there is a saying 'the squeaky wheel gets the grease' – if you get noticed you will be rewarded. In Japan, a parallel saying is 'the nail that sticks up gets hammered down' – if you get noticed it will have a negative effect. In Japan, singling out an individual, even for praise, is negative, whereas in the USA, it is encouraged. From an African perspective behaviour generally is collective, with decisions based on consensus and actions guided by the norms established by the group. Individual ambitions are subservient to group objectives and are kept in check. A typical example is the *chama*, an organised group of men and women in Kenya, who come together for socio-economic support. They raise funds to support each member in turn, and members enforce discipline within the group. The same term is used for a political party where people come together for fundraising or supporting members like a 'merry go round'. Interestingly, the same custom of group socio-economic support is common in the African diaspora in the Caribbean.

Conclusion

OB can be found throughout all types of businesses and other types of organisations. As an employee, supervisor, manager, executive, small business owner or entrepreneur, you will work with others. Understanding behaviour, and how the context influences it, will help improve organisational performance, employee motivation and behaviour and team/group performance; thus, the success and profitability of the business/organisation. This chapter introduced ideas relating to OB and defined several concepts that relate to OB. A particular contextual focus was culture in the African context. Several other related ideas were also outlined.

Review/Discussion

1 Define organisational behaviour in your own terms and identify aspects of OB that you have observed at home, school or work.
2 Identify different forms of organisations and discuss why organisational behaviour is important to each of them.
3 'Owner-managers of small businesses do not need to consider OB' – explain why you agree or disagree with this statement.
4 Explain the factors that inform organisational behaviour in Africa.

Exercise: What's in a Name, Anyway?

Professor Abayomrunkoje Iyare's CV (curriculum vita used for academic resumes) gives his name as Abayomrunkoje (Sunday) Iyare, as he is sometimes called Sunday by close friends and family because he was born on Sunday. He is a well-known Professor of Physics at the University of Nigeria, on sabbatical visiting New York University. He has arrived at his new office and sees that several other faculty members are in their offices. He goes to the next office and sees the name Jennifer Jackson, a name he is familiar with, from the literature. He knocks and enters when a voice says, "come on in".

He says "Jackson, I am Iyare. I have just arrived, and my office is next door".

Professor Jackson replies "Hi Sunday, great to have you here. We've been looking forward to your visit. Please call me Jenny".

Jennifer Jackson is surprised to be called by her last name, but wanting to be friendly, calls the visitor by his familiar name, which she has seen on his CV. She has no idea how to pronounce Abayomrunkoje and is concerned she will mispronounce his name and insult him, so she thinks the use of Sunday is safer.

Professor Iyare is confused by the use of his familiar name by a total stranger, and the lack of formality implied by not using his family name Iyare. He wants to get off to a good start with colleagues in the USA, but he has difficulty calling a woman he has just met 'Jenny'. Further she is a well-known scholar, and the diminutive 'Jenny' seems to be rude.

Assignment

1 Discuss the different backgrounds that each participant comes from.
2 Explain how you think each person should have approached the situation to be more effective.
3 Identify how the participants can move forward so that they build mutual understanding.

References

African Economic Outlook (2019). Retrieved June 2020, from https://www.icafrica.org/en/knowledge-hub/article/african-economic-outlook-2019-362/

Amoako-Agyei, E. (2009). "Cross-cultural management and organisational behaviour in Africa". *Thunderbird International Business Review, 51*, 329–339.

Canadian Journal of Administrative Sciences (2014, Vol. 31, no.4)

Gilder Lehrman Institute of American History. (n.d.). Retrieved December 22, 2020, from https://www.gilderlehrman.org/history-resources/teaching-resource/historical-context-facts-about-slave-trade-and-slavery

Hofstede, G. (1980, 2001). *Culture's consequences*. Beverley Hills, CA: Sage. Retrieved from https://geerthofstede.com/culture-geert-hofstede-gert-jan-hofstede/6d-model-of-national-culture/

House, R. J., Hanges, P. J., Javidan, M., Dorfman, P. W., & Gupta, V. (Eds.). (2004). *Culture, leadership, and organizations: The GLOBE study of 62 societies*. Thousand Oaks, CA: Sage Publications.

Jackson, T. (2004). *Management and change in Africa: A cross-cultural perspective*. London: Routledge.

Mnyaka, M., & Motlhabi, M. (2005). "The African concept of *Ubuntu/ Botho* and its socio-moral significance". *Black Theology*, *3*(2), 215–237.

Ncube, L. B. (2010). "Ubuntu: A transformative leadership philosophy". *Journal of Leadership Studies*, *4*(3), 77–82. DOI: **10.1002/jls.20182**

Noorderhaven, N., & Tidjani, B. (2001). "Culture, governance and economic performance: An explorative study with a special focus on Africa". *International Journal of Cross Cultural Management*, *1*(1), 31–52.

Punnett, B. J. (2019). *International perspectives on organizational behavior*. London: Routledge.

Schwartz, S. H. (1992). Universals in the content and structure of values: Theory and empirical tests in 20 countries. In M. Zanna (Ed.), *Advances in experimental social psychology* (Vol. 25, pp. 1–65). New York, NY: Academic Press.

Tangpong, C., Li, J., Hung, K., & Senaji, T. (2012). "The effect of reciprocity norm on ethical compromise: A cross-cultural investigation". *Proceedings of the 43rd annual meeting of the decision sciences institute*, November 2012, San Francisco, CA.

Trompenaars, F., & Hampden-Turner, C. (1998). *Riding the waves of culture: Understanding cultural diversity in global business* (2nd ed). New York, NY: McGraw-Hill.

Tutu, D. M. (2004). *God has a dream: A vision of hope for our time*. London: Rider.

Wanasika, I., Howell, J. P., Littrell, R., & Dorfman, P. (2011). "Managerial leadership and culture in sub-Saharan Africa". *Journal of World Business*, *46*, 234–241.

World Values Survey (2018). Retrieved from http://worldvaluessurvey.org

2 Personal/Individual Factors

Learning Outcomes

After completing this chapter, you will be able to:

- Define personality and explain how it affects work behaviour
- Describe/contrast the Big Five personality traits
- Explain the importance of personality at work
- Discuss self-monitoring and impression management
- Explain perception and perceptual biases
- Define values and attitudes, and discuss how they relate to each other
- Discuss the role of emotions and emotional intelligence in behaviour
- Discuss personal/individual factors in the African context

Thought Starters

You visit a workplace, observe activities and think that you can improve it. Among the Swahili on the Kenyan coast, the Somali from the north-east and the Eastleigh Estate of Nairobi, people eat rice from the same plate using their fingers. You may think "Oh, they need spoons and forks". If you made a 'philanthropic gesture' of purchasing cutlery for them, you would be surprised when you returned to find them still eating with their fingers, with the new cutlery carefully placed next to the plate.

What you think you see is not always reality ….

There is a story that each of two shoe companies sent a salesman to Africa in the early 1900s. One returned to North America and said "they don't wear shoes, there is no market". The second returned and

DOI: 10.4324/9781003036838-2

said, "they don't wear shoes, the market is enormous". The second was the Canadian Bata Shoe Company and 'Bata' has become synonymous with 'shoe' in many parts of Africa.

How you interpret reality depends on many things ....

Summary

This chapter discusses individual characteristics at work. It considers personality, personality types and their assessment; how we manage the impression others have of us, perception and perceptual mistakes/biases, values and attitudes, the role of emotions in behaviour and the concept of emotional intelligence. These are explored relative to managing individual characteristics to improve individual and overall organisational performance. Throughout we consider the African context and how these characteristics are likely to be affected by this.

Introduction

Individuals are the core of all organisations; it is often said that people are an organisation's most important resource. Even with increased automation, organisations rely on people to design machines, ensure they perform as required and work alongside them. In African countries, much work takes place informally and in small/medium sized enterprises (SMEs); thus, people are crucial to performance as automation is expensive and more likely in larger organisations. It is important to understand why people behave the way they do, especially in this context. We focus on individual characteristics likely to influence people's behaviour. Figure 2.1 displays factors affecting behaviour and organisational effectiveness. It highlights individual and group needs, attitudes and norms, how culture affects these, and how these result in behaviours related to effectiveness.

We now consider a variety of personal factors.

Personality

Personality refers to qualities that form an individual's distinctive character – "she has a comely personality that is engaging" or "he had an abrasive personality making it difficult to like him". Personality explains a person's characteristics, thoughts, emotions and behaviours – a collection of traits that affect how a person is perceived. There are various traits used to describe personality. We used

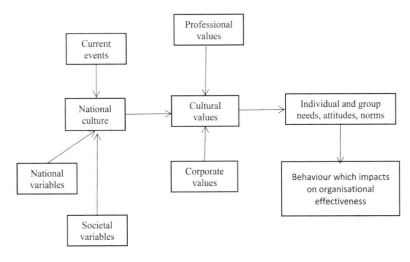

Figure 2.1 Relating Culture to Business/Management.

'comely' and 'abrasive'. Research has classified these traits into five dimensions called 'The Big Five':

- *Conscientiousness* – dependable, organised, reliable and hardworking. People high on conscientious are organised, mindful of details, plan, think about the impact of behaviour and are mindful of deadlines. Those low on conscientiousness dislike structures/schedules, act on the spur of the moment or procrastinate, may be messy.
- *Agreeableness* – kindness, cooperation and helpfulness. People high in agreeableness are cooperative, empathetic, care about others. Those low on this are competitive, sometimes manipulative, have less interest in others.
- *Neuroticism* – nervousness, mood changes, emotional instability, jealousy. People high on this experience mood swings, anxiety, irritability, often feel stressed. Those low are stable, emotionally resilient, relaxed.
- *Openness to experience* – curiosity, imagination, creativity. People high on this are adventurous, innovative. People low are more traditional, have difficulty with abstractions.
- *Extraversion* – talkative, sociable, assertive, dominant. People high on extraversion are outgoing, enjoy social situations, being around others excites them. Those low in extraversion (or introverted) are reserved, less energetic in social settings, preferring the life of the inner mind over the outer world of others.

Traits are described/measured on a scale from very high to very low. Most people are somewhere between, combining different characteristics. Longitudinal studies suggest that traits are relatively stable, although people become less extraverted, less neurotic, less open to experience and more agreeable and conscientious as they age (Marsh, Nagengast, & Morin, 2013). Given the young workforce in many African countries, one might expect them to be relatively extraverted, neurotic and open to experience, and somewhat lower on agreeableness and conscientiousness. This should be considered at work. Low agreeableness may have negative implications for teamwork while low conscientiousness can significantly affect meeting goals and deadlines. Effective oversight would be appropriate to deal with these traits. African cultures are believed to listen to/revere older people, and this can be used to offset some of the challenges posed by the former personality descriptors. Positively, young employees will be open to new experiences, are creative and enjoy interacting with others. These can be an advantage, particularly in today's fast changing environment.

McCrae and, Terracciano's Personality Profiles of Cultures Project (2005) found that the big five traits are essentially universal. People from more than 50 cultures exhibited the five dimensions. The types may be universal, but the view of what is positive may be influenced by culture. In the West, extroversion is often seen as positive, while in the East introversion is viewed more positively. The African context is closer to the East in that extraversion may be interpreted as boastfulness, indicating 'you think you know more than anyone else'. Some researchers argue that aspects of certain cultures are not captured by the model. Ashton et al. (2004) building on the Big Five, adds Honesty-Humility (high honesty-humility – straightforward, modest, fair; low – deceitful, boastful). Humility and honesty are highly valued in most African cultures and lacking this trait frowned upon. In addition, sentimentality/toughness is added to the Neuroticism trait (renamed Emotionality) and anger/even-tempered is associated with Agreeableness.

Personality is seen as an important way of understanding organisational behaviour; for example:

• Matching employees and jobs. Some jobs require creativity while others depend on closely following required policies/procedures. Some jobs include close interactions with others and the need to be agreeable, while others are completed with virtually no interactions.

- Providing behavioural training geared to aspects of personality which could cause problems. Someone high on neuroticism/ emotionalism may need help with stressful situations.
- Helping understand and react to various behaviours. If someone is an introvert, we do not expect them to be talkative and social at work.

Interestingly, people can train themselves to deal with situations that are not comfortable for their personality type. Many academics describe themselves as introverts, yet in class and other social situations they appear like extroverts, when required, by performing/ acting.

Behaviour is a function of both underlying personality and situational variables, although people generally behave consistent with these underlying traits. Some personality traits seem inherently good at one extreme and undesirable at the other. For example, honesty/ humility seems desirable, while deceit/boasting does not. We should not, however, think of one personality type as better than another. It may simply be better in a particular situation. Even with honesty/ humility, there may be situations that are better handled by not being honest or humble. In Africa, generally, honesty/humility is seen as desirable and virtuous.

The preferred personality type at work depends on the work to be performed and the needed interactions with others. COVID-19 means that the world of work has changed, with more people working remotely rather than together in offices. Many people believe this will continue, at least to some degree. It is not entirely clear how personality impacts this type of work, but it may be a relevant individual factor. Research in this area is just starting and there is anecdotal evidence that some people react well to and are productive working remotely, while others are the opposite. It seems likely that personality is one of the variables that explains the difference.

Personality assessment is used by some organisations as part of the hiring process and to match individuals to jobs, as well as to determine promotion and training and development needs. If one wants to use personality assessment effectively in organisations, careful thought needs to be given to the interplay between personality and the work/workplace because the workplace demands on personality vary. There are many instruments that measure personality that have been used relatively widely for some time in the West. In that context they are considered reliable (scores will be consistent from test to test and over time) and valid (results provide useful information and if a person scores high on extroversion, they behave like an extrovert). These measures have not been tested extensively in African countries, so we cannot say with certainty that they are equally reliable and valid in Africa. Organisations in Africa using personality assessment will therefore want to be cautious in their use and monitor the results of such tests. Studies should explore the reliability and validity of these assessment tools with African samples to enable their adaptation to this context.

Whatever a person's innate personality is like, we all seek to manage how we appear to others to create a desired impression. We monitor our behaviour so that others see us as we want to be seen.

Impression Management/Self-Monitoring

Impression management is a conscious or subconscious process to influence others' perceptions about ourselves, others, objects or events, usually by controlling information. Most often it means attempting to control others' thinking about us through self-monitoring. We behave in ways we think show us in a certain light, usually positive. If the supervisor is in the room, most people try to show they are working hard, helping others and so on. If someone meets a potential employer at a party, most people behave in ways they think the employer will find attractive, express interest in the company and so on. Self-monitoring and impression management may mean we behave in ways contrary to our innate personality – if normally introverted, we try to be more extroverted at the party; if not usually agreeable, we try to be more helpful in the office situation.

Self-monitoring/impression management has positive and negative consequences at work. On the positive side, people with less desirable traits or behaviours for a particular workplace manage these and improve the impression they make on others. People can be coached/trained to manage undesirable characteristics or behaviours, and desired ones can be rewarded/reinforced. On the negative side, people cover up undesirable traits/behaviours in the short-term to obtain desired outcomes, but in the longer term, they may revert to their more basic character. Supervisors, co-workers, subordinates may be misled by self-monitoring/impression management. The individual can also be hurt by creating a particular impression, as it can cause stress to pretend to be something false/unfamiliar.

In organisations, self-monitoring/impression management takes place all the time. These seem to be universal behaviours across African countries as elsewhere; however, the specific choices of what makes a good impression will be affected by culture – for example, in an African country, being respectful towards your elders is positive and someone might show such respect to give a positive impression. Self-presentation can be important to landing a job, and employees want to show the right image to superiors, colleagues and subordinates to be liked, seen as competent and committed and get rewards and promotions. Managers want to ensure they are not misled by these behaviours, but they also want to encourage them when they result in desired outcomes. Impression management is about how others perceive us; so next we look at the concept of perception.

Perception

Perception is a cognitive process allowing interpretation of the stimuli in the environment around us. We are selective in perceptions and how we organise them to interpret the situation. Imagine entering a room full of people for the first time – your brain would be overwhelmed if you tried to take in all the details of the room and the people, so instead it selects certain features and organises them into something meaningful. What we select depends on the characteristics of objects – intensity, size, contrast, repetition, motion, novelty/familiarity – and our motivation, emotions, values, personality. Essentially, we perceive what is likely to affect us. After the selective process, the brain organises stimuli into something meaningful. As a lecturer, when I enter a classroom I 'see' (perceive) the things that affect my ability to lecture – the arrangement of seats/desks, the location of the white board, podium, computer, projector, etc.; also, anything unusual/unexpected, say a piano in the middle of the room, a straw figure hanging in the corner. I do not notice many other things, such as lights, wall colour, flooring, etc. (unless my attention is drawn to them for some reason).

The process of perception is universal; all people perceive things around them and select those they want to organise into meaning. The underlying process is universal because of the nature of the human mind, but the specifics may differ in different locations. Using the lecturer example, certain features of a classroom may be common in Africa and uncommon in North America or the Middle East, students may behave differently, lectures may take various forms and so on – these would all influence one's perceptions and consequently behaviours.

The nature of perception means different people can perceive the same information differently. It is common that people hear what they want to hear and ignore information that is contrary to what they believe. We think there is an objective reality for everyone, but this is not always the case. Think of a major event in your life and ask someone who experienced it with you to describe it, you will find that your memory and theirs varies substantially. This is relevant in the workplace, because it can lead to misperceptions and misunderstandings and these can cause conflict. At work, perception checking is vital, particularly regarding important matters, and includes:

- Repetition – give information more than once, using different words.
- Feedback – ask receivers of information to respond.
- Clarification – ask for and give answers to anything unclear.
- Media – use a variety of media (e.g., follow a verbal message with a written one).
- Fact checking – check assumptions and look for facts.
- Self-knowledge – know your own biases and how they affect your perceptions.

Some common perceptual biases have been identified:

- Attribution – the tendency to consider positive behaviours/results 'internal' to oneself, and negative ones 'external'. If I receive a high mark, I can attribute this to my hard work (internal) or to the fact that the lecturer gave an easy exam (external). In Western countries, particularly English-speaking ones, it is typical to attribute positive results internally and negative ones externally.
- Culture – the tendency to interpret things from your own cultural perspective. People in individualist cultures value individuals, personal goals and independence; so these attributes are perceived as positive. Collectivist cultures see individuals as members of groups such as families, tribes, work units and so on and are more likely to value conformity and interdependence.
- Stereotyping – the tendency to attribute certain characteristics to all members of a particular group, and explain behaviours/situations based on this. If we believe all Americans are loud and we see an American shouting, we assume it is because they are American. In reality, they may be shouting to get our attention because of danger.
- Self-serving – the tendency to perceive behaviours and situations in a way that allows us to maintain and enhance our self-esteem and to perceive ourselves in a favourable manner. The reverse may also occur where someone sees themselves in a negative light.

- Belief – the tendency to make judgements on the basis of one's beliefs. If you agree with a viewpoint, you are more likely to believe arguments that lead to the conclusion you believe in, and less likely to question the facts that lead to this conclusion.
- Selectivity – the tendency not to notice, and more quickly forget, stimuli that cause emotional discomfort and contradict prior beliefs.

To avoid perceptual biases and consequent mistakes, you need to be aware of them in yourself and in others. It is necessary to fact-check assumptions, particularly when dealing with important issues at work. Perceptions are influenced by values and attitudes as well as emotions, discussed next.

Values/Attitudes

Values and attitudes are closely related to a person's character and personality. Both are fundamental to behaviour in organisations. They are inter-related concepts; however, there is a distinction between them.

Values can be defined as fundamental principles guiding attitudes/ actions. Values are also part of ethics. These are complex subjects and we do not discuss them in any depth but simply give a brief explanation of how they develop and what they mean to behaviour. Certain values may be innate, but we usually think of learning values from parents, family, schools, religious organisations and other sources such as professional societies. Values determine what we consider right and wrong. Universally good values are kindness, honesty, love, compassion, justice and the like; universally bad are murder, rape, sex with a child, hate and so on. Other values are more local and often related to culture – the role of women in society, acceptable ways of dressing, religious practices.

At work, values and ethics focus on institution-related practices and are often codified in a code of conduct outlining standards of behaviour for employees. These values are usually codified as 'core values' and communicated throughout the workplace to guide members' actions. They can cover an array of issues such as use of company property, behaviour towards co-workers, management/employee relationships, making illegal payments, time off for charitable work, environmental actions, to mention a few. These codes demonstrate what is considered 'good' and 'bad' within the company. Organisational members are expected to behave in ways consistent with the values;

and appropriate sanctions are applied for not acting in accordance with them.

Attitudes are mental and emotional states within a person that affect reactions to oneself, others, places, things or events. They are complex and are acquired through experiences. Attitudes involve judgments about an object, subject matter or person. They are personal responses and thus differ among people. When we think of fundamentally universal values, we expect attitudes to be similar across people – if most people value life and think taking another's life is wrong, most people will have a negative attitude towards murder. Even in this extreme example, there may be situations where taking a life is not considered negative; for example, a mother protecting her children might be seen as brave and elicit a positive attitude towards her. When we think of values that vary across locations and cultures, we expect attitudes to be similar within a group and to differ across groups. If women are expected to cover their face and head in a particular society, an uncovered woman will be viewed negatively, while in another, a covered woman might be viewed negatively.

Attitudes are affected by more than values, including personality, perceptions, emotions and so on. A colleague grew up where there were many 'night lizards' (grey lizards seen only at night) and was told they could stick to her skin and a hot iron was needed to get them off. Further, if she misbehaved, a night lizard would be caught and put on her arm. As an adult, she knows lizards are good for the environment, and she values them, but she has an instinctive revulsion to them and retains a negative attitude towards them. Her attitude is not based on reason but on emotion. In the workplace, similar things affect attitudes. If we had a boss of a certain gender who was difficult to work with, we might have a negative attitude towards any boss of that gender. Workplace attitudes often develop based on the norms in a particular company. Some companies are accepting of employees using corporate supplies, such as pens, pencils, pads, paper and so on, and the attitude to taking these home is neutral or positive; in others this is frowned on as the equivalent of stealing, and attitudes are negative.

Companies want to encourage attitudes, such as commitment, that will be beneficial to the workplace and workforce productivity and can do so in several ways. They can make clear what is acceptable and positive. If the company wants to discourage taking supplies home, the negative impact on the company can be explained and each employee can be allocated a certain number of pens, etc. Positive attitudes can be rewarded and negative ones can be sanctioned. If a company wants to ensure attendance, rewards can be linked to being at work on time.

Training and development programmes can be used to deal with dysfunctional workplace attitudes. If a company wants to create an equitable organisational culture, programmes focusing on equality can be implemented. Changing attitudes is not easy, as in the lizard example, and effective change of any kind starts at the top. Top management must exhibit desired attitudes and behaviours if they are to be adopted elsewhere in the organisation.

In a study commissioned by the East Africa Institute of the Aga Khan University, a total of 7000 individuals in the age group of 18–35 years, in Kenya, Uganda, Tanzania and Rwanda, were interviewed between 2014 and 2015 to examine their thinking about themselves and their values and attitudes. The estimated median age in East Africa is about 17 years, and East Africa is one of the youngest regions in the world (median age is about 40 in Europe, 38 in North America, 29 in Asia). Census data for the countries studied identify about 80% of the population as below 35 years.

Respondents saw themselves first as young people (40%), then as citizens of their countries (34%), 11% identified their faith first and 6% as members of their family. Only 3.5% reported their tribe/ethnicity as the first dimension of their identity. This is an important finding, suggesting that tribe/ethnicity is playing a small part in young people's perceptions of themselves. Being young, in contrast, is important and can be built on in the workplace. In Kenya, the proportion of young people who identified by ethnicity was 4% in the age group of 18 and 20 years and nearly doubled to 7.8% in the age group of 21 and 35 years. In Tanzania ethnicity remained essentially the same across ages.

About 80% of those surveyed valued faith the most, about half valued work and family, 37% valued wealth and a quarter freedom. About 60% admired those involved in 'get-rich-quick' schemes; more than half believed it didn't matter how one makes money and 53% said they would 'do anything' to get money. The survey found 37% would take or give a bribe and 35% believed there is nothing wrong with corruption. Rwanda was different, where most respondents would not take or give a bribe and believed corruption was wrong. The findings point to a value system that breeds unwanted attitudes towards bribes and corruption and 'get rich quickly without work'. Particularly disturbing is the belief that 'it does not matter how one makes money'. This is contrary to religious teachings and the finding that '80% valued faith most'. It seems the religious faith of 80% does not translate to moral values. These findings suggest positive attitudes towards corruption and bribes; hence, a propensity to pilfer or steal and other antisocial behaviours including doing anything to make money. This suggests a need for programmes to train staff against these behaviours and to inculcate more positive values and attitudes so that youth appreciate the value of work and sound moral principles.

Emotions/Emotional Intelligence

Emotions are relatively short-lived feelings formed in reaction to particular events. We may be happy because the sun has come out, bored because our project seems to have stalled, sad because someone is unwell and so on. Emotions are based on internal feelings, although they may be expressed externally. If we are angry, that is internal, but if we shout at someone, we are expressing our anger. In the business world, emotions can have a major impact on employees' morale, productivity and job performance. Managers want to create and support a positive emotional work experience and avoid a negative one.

Positive emotions include feeling calm, comfortable, energetic, enthusiastic, excited, happy, joyful, peaceful, relaxed, satisfied, loved and cared for. Research suggests that the most positive emotions at work are feeling comfortable, satisfied, enthusiastic and valued at work. Negative emotions include feeling annoyed, anxious, bored, disinterested, dissatisfied, frustrated, gloomy, miserable, sad, stressed, tired, uncomfortable, unhappy, upset and worried. The top negative emotions at work are frustration, stress and anxiety. Employees can also feel moral emotions like guilt, regret and shame; the most negative moral emotions are humiliation, disgust and resentment.

The challenge for managers is to create an environment that encourages the positive emotions and discourages/manages the negative ones. Generally, a trusting environment contributes positively because people feel comfortable expressing their emotions and this helps deal with them. Employees who feel that they are treated fairly and are interested in their work tend to be more satisfied and this in turn contributes to positive emotions. The work environment should be designed in a manner that elicits positive emotions and managers should endeavour to support employees emotionally when need arises, say, during job cuts, salary cuts and the loss of a relative or colleague. The importance of managing emotions at work has led to the concept of emotional intelligence.

Emotional Intelligence

Emotional intelligence has become a popular concept in the past 20 years. It refers to the ability to recognise one's own emotions and those of others, distinguish among different feelings, use information on emotions in thinking and behaviour and adjust emotions to different environments. Goleman's (1995) model of emotional intelligence includes know your emotions, manage your emotions, motivate yourself, recognise and understand other people's emotions. These are broken down into four quadrants: self-awareness, social awareness, self-management and relationship management. Emotional intelligence can be described as:

Self-awareness – be conscious of your own feelings and motives; knowing how your emotions affect you and others, not allowing your emotions to control you.

Self-regulation – avoid making impulsive decisions; take time to think about the consequences of an action before acting.

Motivation – be productive; assessing how your actions will contribute to long-term success.

Empathy – avoid being self-centred; empathise with others, be a good listener, slow to judge, understanding the needs/wants of others.

Social skills – like to collaborate, work in teams; be considered a good leader because of communication skills and ability to manage relationships.

Emotional intelligence is a beneficial individual characteristic for both managers and employees. There are several tests designed to measure emotional intelligence that can be helpful for self-evaluation as well as assessment by a company. We have not found any evidence of their use in African contexts and cannot say whether they will be reliable or valid. Many people, however, find it interesting to do a self-test to gauge their personal emotional intelligence (these tests can be found online for those interested). There are some findings on its relationship to performance in organisations in the West, but this relationship has not been established in the African context and remains an area of scholarly interest. For those not naturally emotionally intelligent, it is possible to cultivate this intelligence by reflecting on one's emotions and emotional responses. In addition, continuous development programmes can be implemented to improve the emotional intelligence of organisational members.

Conclusion

This chapter considered individual and personal characteristics that affect work behaviour. It examined personality and personality types, self-monitoring and impression management, perception and perceptual biases, values and attitudes and the role of emotions and emotional intelligence. Where possible, these topics were considered from the African context. There is little research that specifically focuses on Africa relative to these topics and it is important for readers to think about the material presented and ask how these concepts apply in African countries.

Review/Discussion

1 Discuss the values that organisations should embrace amid crises such as pandemics and disasters with respect to their employees.
2 Consider how emotional intelligence can be improved in your team/group or leaders.
3 Evaluate the following: 'Undesirable personality traits can be used as a means for improving performance in an organisation'.
4 Identify and explain a concept that you perceive as important based on the discussions in this chapter.

Exercise: Managing Personality

Mr. Otieno is a high performer who consistently meets management's expectations. The majority of co-workers in the department think that Mr. Otieno is neurotic and avoid dealing with him if possible. Mr. Kibet is one of his close friends, and wants to approach him to explain the concerns of their co-workers; however, he is not sure how Mr. Otieno will react.

Assignment

1 How do you think this situation should be handled to avoid a negative reaction from Mr. Otieno?
2 If Mr. Kibet speaks to Mr. Otieno, what effect is likely, at the individual and team level, and for the organisation at large?
3 If you were Mr. Otieno, would you like your friend to discuss this with you? Why? Why not?

References

Ashton, M. C., Lee, K., Perugini, M., Szarota, P., de Vries, R. E., Di Blas, L. ... De Raad, B. (2004). "A six-factor structure of personality-descriptive adjectives: Solutions from psycholexical studies in seven languages". *Journal of Personality and Social Psychology*, *86*(2), 356–366.
Goleman, D. (1995). *Emotional intelligence*. New York, NY: Bantam Books.

Marsh, H. W., Nagengast, B., & Morin, A. J. S. (2013). "Measurement invariance of big-five factors over the lifespan: ESEM tests of gender, age, plasticity, maturity, and la dolce vita effects". *Developmental Psychology*, 49(6), 1194–1218.

McCrae, R. R., Terracciano, A., & Personality Profiles of Cultures Project. (2005). "Universal features of personality traits from the observer's perspective: Data from 50 different cultures". *Journal of Personality and Social Psychology*, 88, 547–561.

3 Job Performance and Job Design

Learning Objectives

After completing this chapter, you will be able to:

- Explain job and task performance
- Describe the job characteristics model and discuss its components
- Discuss occupational health and safety, including mental health
- Describe alternative work arrangements
- Explain the causes and outcomes of job satisfaction
- Discuss organisational commitment, citizenship behaviours, counterproductive work behaviours
- Explain the role of the family and the concept of work-life balance
- Discuss how these concepts apply in the African context

Thought Starters

The workers were building my new house, it was not big, but was three stories high, and the drop from the top to the ground could kill someone and would certainly injure anyone who fell. From time to time, we visited to see the progress. There would be workers on the top floor, no safety harnesses or lines and the site smelled of marijuana/bhang (cannabis sativa). I was terrified someone would get hurt. When I asked the contractor, he said 'don't worry', 'they know what they are doing', 'they always get high before they go up high'. No-one got hurt happily, but the idea still worries me.

Summary

This chapter considers aspects of the job that influence behaviour/ performance. Characteristics of jobs/tasks, issues associated with health at work, different work arrangements, are considered in terms of their relationship to motivation, satisfaction, performance and

DOI: 10.4324/9781003036838-3

commitment to the organisation. Organisational citizenship behaviours that positively affect work and counterproductive behaviours that negatively affect work are explained. Finally, we consider the role of the family and work-life balance. Throughout, we consider how the African context is likely to influence these factors.

Job Analysis/Descriptions

A job is usually outlined in a *job description* specifying the tasks and duties that make up the job, the outcomes expected, the responsibilities and authority associated with the job and reporting relationships. It includes specification of the qualifications and skills required to do the job, and the benefits associated with it. A job description is important for both employer and employee. It provides the employee with a clear idea of what is required to satisfactorily perform the job, and it assures the employer that all necessary tasks and duties have been covered. This is an ideal situation as there are always unforeseen tasks/duties that arise.

Organisations begin with a *job analysis*, identifying tasks to be completed to achieve some output, grouping these tasks, assessing the time needed to complete them, then defining 'jobs' on this basis. This forms the basis for job descriptions. Job analysis is done by larger companies and government departments but is unusual in smaller organisations. In small organisations, and even medium sized ones, there is often a general sense of what is required to do a job – e.g., a cleaner in a restaurant 'spends about two hours sweeping out and mopping the main room morning and evening (total 4 hours), one hour on the washrooms twice a day (total 2 hours), 15 minutes per table after guests leave (total 2 hours)' which serves as the basis for their job description. The description could be formal and written or informal and verbally explained. In smaller organisations, it is likely to be accompanied by 'other duties', such as, 'the cleaner will be required to assist in the kitchen as required'. Smaller organisations, of which there are many in African countries, may treat job descriptions informally, but this does not negate their importance. Employees need to know what is expected of them, and employers need to be sure that all necessary tasks/duties are covered. A job will be performed effectively when the tasks required are clearly specified hence clarity of the job description/expected performance is critical.

Job Characteristics Model

This model considers how jobs can be designed to make them motivating and satisfying. It looks at aspects of the job and asks, 'could we make it more intrinsically (internally) interesting?' In the example of a restaurant cleaner, 'would the job be more motivating if the cleaner did other jobs from time to time?', 'had responsibility to check on the quality of cleanliness?', 'received feedback from customers on cleanliness?' and so on. Where jobs are repetitive and essentially 'boring', the job characteristics model suggests they can be made more interesting, and more motivating, by focusing on certain characteristics.

In the early 1900s, following the industrial revolution, job design focused on simplifying jobs, having workers specialise in one or a few tasks which they could do well. Industrial psychologists in the mid-1900s concluded that this type of work did not motivate workers. This led to the idea of incorporating more variety into work, through *job enlargement and rotation*; a worker could produce a 'widget' and check its quality (enlargement) or work on producing 'widgets' for a period then move to making 'pidgets', then stock taking, quality control and so on (rotation). This allows the worker to learn new tasks and adds variety to the job/work. Further study suggested that there was more to increasing motivation than simply variety and focused on *job enrichment.*

The main components are based on Hackman and Oldham (1976), and depict job characteristic related to psychological states resulting in high motivation, satisfaction and performance as follows.

Job Characteristics (1), Psychological States (2), Work Outcomes (3)

(1) Skill Variety, Task Identity, Task Significance lead to (2) Experienced Meaningfulness
(1) Autonomy leads to (2) Experienced Responsibility for Work Outcomes
(1) Feedback leads to (2) Experienced Knowledge of Results
(2) Meaningfulness, Responsibility, Knowledge lead to (3) High Motivation/Satisfaction/Performance

Skill variety refers to the degree to which a job demands different activities in the execution of the tasks, where various skills and talents are used. *Task identity* is the degree to which the work demands a complete process or product, so that a certain job has a clear beginning and ending, allowing a person to work on a complete process/product rather than small parts. *Task significance* relates to a sense that the job has a substantial impact on the lives of other people within the organisation and on society. *Autonomy* is the degree to which an employee can work independently. *Feedback* relates to an employee's understanding of the effectiveness of their performance. Feedback is mainly provided by the supervisor but also by peers, and sometimes customers, users and others.

Using this model, a **Motivational Potential Score** (MPS) can be calculated: MPS = (skill variety + task identity + task significance)/ 3 * autonomy * feedback. The greater the skill variety, task identity/ significance, autonomy and feedback, the more motivating a job is, and this is accompanied by high levels of satisfaction/performance. This model appeals to people whose growth needs are high and who have the requisite skills, knowledge and abilities to perform a variety of tasks and accept a degree of autonomy.

Employees at higher levels in African organisations are likely to react positively to jobs that are identified as having a high MPS; they will be motivated by variety, task identity, significance and so on. Organisations should evaluate the work content of these jobs to see how they can be designed to improve these factors. Some organisations in African countries, however, may be dealing with unskilled employees who may be largely concerned with producing at a specified level. These employees may prefer to learn one skill and be able to perform that skill quickly and easily; they may not want variety or task identity. They may be making parts for machines that are unfamiliar and may not be able to appreciate task significance. These employees may believe that managers are in their positions to make decisions and may not want responsibility associated with autonomy. For these employees, job enrichment might be de-motivating rather than motivating. Job enrichment may be interpreted as being 'set up for failure'. We believe that feedback is important in any context, and that employees should always receive feedback on their performance.

The USA is individualistic and moderate on uncertainty avoidance, while African countries are more collective and relatively high on uncertainty avoidance. The job characteristics model is likely effective in countries with a similar cultural profile to that of the USA. More collective societies may be more motivated by opportunities to interact with colleagues in their cohort than by their individual experience; higher uncertainty avoidance societies may feel that job variety and autonomy provide uncertainty. African societies may also be more receptive to power differences, and this would imply that decisions should be made by those in positions of power with subordinates accepting and carrying out these decisions.

Today's employees are likely to be more educated and familiar with new technologies. These changes may mean that the job design components advocated by the job characteristics model are more relevant to these employees and provide a motivating job environment. Managers in African countries should carefully consider the design of jobs in this context to ensure that jobs provide motivating potential. If an employer in Africa wants to develop jobs based on this model, it may be necessary to provide training for employees to help them understand the underlying concepts. The next section considers occupational health and safety.

Occupational Health and Safety

Most people spend a substantial portion of time working. Typically, 6–8 hours are spent asleep, 6–8 hours in personal activities (shopping, gardening, preparing meals, eating and so on) and 8–10 getting to/from work and working. This means experiences at work influence our physical and mental health. In turn, our health influences our performance on the job, including our efficiency/productivity and effectiveness, and relationships with others.

First, consider the physical aspects of occupations. Some jobs are demanding, requiring hours of standing, moving, lifting heavy objects and so on. Abilities should be matched to job requirements. Even then, they have the potential for physical overextension and even injury and this needs to be factored into work days, including appropriate breaks, to limit the likelihood of negative consequences. A worker who cannot work because of exhaustion or injury may be costing the company in other ways as well, such as sick pay, workplace compensation, etc. This can also have a negative effect on co-workers. At the other extreme, some jobs require no physical activity, and someone completes the work sitting throughout the day. This can also have negative consequences and workers need the opportunity to move around and be active regularly, and this needs to be factored into the work day. Some jobs require repetitive movements, such as twisting wires in a certain way, over and over, or repeating certain stitches or cutting motions, and these can lead to physical injuries – most common is carpel tunnel, which affects the wrist and makes using the hand difficult and painful.

Jobs in mining, construction, forestry, fishing, agriculture and the like fall into the first category in terms of physical issues. These jobs are common in many African countries; therefore, it is important for management to ensure that they are carried out safely. A concern for managers is that employers and employees alike may be accustomed to taking risks in these industries and accidents may be considered relatively acceptable. This poses a challenge when safety measures are imposed. Risk-taking is considered a source of (manly) pride and safety measures are the reverse. However, these measures may be critical to keeping people at work and productive. Management will often need to provide training programmes to overcome resistance, and to put incentives in place to encourage a safe workplace. Secretarial jobs, assembly jobs, clothing manufacture and similar jobs fall into the second category of repetitive injury. These jobs are often held by women who are likely to be more risk averse. They may relate positively to management's attempts to avoid injury, and this can make change easier than in the former case.

Health issues include emotional and mental conditions. These are often harder to identify than physical ones, but can be equally detrimental to performance and productivity. The fact that they are hard to identify makes them especially important for managers whose goal is fostering a productive workforce. Emotional and mental issues can be caused by personal issues outside of work, or can be the result of job and workplace conditions. Managers need to monitor employees for signs of emotional or mental distress and deal with such signs quickly. If the cause of the distress is outside of work, managers can be supportive and helpful in finding outside help. If the cause is in the workplace then the manager is more directly responsible for identifying causes and finding solutions. In broad terms, we talk of workplace stress and its causes and outcomes. The following outlines these.

Stress is a state of mental or emotional strain/tension resulting from adverse/demanding circumstances. In the workplace, the causes of stress range from underutilisation of abilities and having too little to do, to the reverse, too much work and work that is too difficult. The main causes of stress are:

- **The people at work** – if employees cannot work well together; they have differing values, attitudes, personalities and so on, blame others when things go wrong, have varying perceptions of what is expected and what constitutes good performance – these can cause conflict and stress.
- **The work environment** – if it is unpleasant; too hot, cold, cramped, bad lighting, incorrect tools and so on – these physical aspects can cause stress, particularly when they cannot be changed, and employees feel powerless to affect the situation.
- **The job itself** – if it is wrong; an employee is underqualified or overqualified, has the wrong skills, lacks interest in the job, has ethical concerns and so on – these intrinsic aspects of the work can be stressful and mentally draining.

- **Negative employer-employee relations** – if these are confrontational; supervision is constant or non-existent, punishment for infractions seems harsh, wages/benefits unfair and so on – these negative relationships cause stress.

Stress is inevitable at work and some stress is usually positive; however, beyond a certain level, the consequences are negative. Too much stress results in an unpleasant workplace, this leads to absenteeism and turnover as well as lower productivity. Stress also leads to additional stressors. For example, too much work leads to people feeling anxious and this can result in arguments and conflict, and other undesirable results. Stress is not just mental, it has physical consequences, including headaches, high blood pressure and sleeplessness. Stress over time can lead to more serious diseases such as strokes, heart attacks and diabetes. Managing stress at work is therefore essential.

Managing Stress

Where stress is dysfunctional it is important to manage it. The first step is to identify the cause(s) of stress for a particular person/group or job(s). Once the causes are identified, then solutions can be considered and carefully implemented, and the results can be monitored. If conflict within a group is the cause of stress; and if the cause is identified as unclear roles within the group then roles can be defined more clearly for each member of the group. Alternatively, if the cause is identified as religious differences, the solution will be quite different, perhaps diversity training for the group plus individual counselling.

In companies in Africa, workplace stress is likely to be as great a cause for concern as elsewhere. The reasons for stress are also likely to be similar; that is, too much or too little work, conflict, uncertainty and so on. The solutions considered may, however, vary from place to place and organisation to organisation. For example, cultural values may be important. In more collective cultures, the group may be the focus (e.g., counselling or training for co-workers in a group setting versus one-on-one counselling or training). Where avoiding uncertainty is important, flexible roles and policies/procedures may cause stress, and adding clarity will help. Where managers are expected to make decisions, asking subordinates to take on this added responsibility will be stressful, and if this is desired, it will need to be accompanied by training and support.

Ways of dealing with stress may also involve alternate work arrangements. In the past, it has been traditional that employees go to a place of work, a factory, an office and so on, and are expected to arrive at a certain time and leave at a certain time, having completed the requisite number of hours. These work arrangements have been changing more recently, and the COVID-19 pandemic has encouraged thinking about alternate arrangements.

Alternative Work Arrangements

It has become increasingly apparent in the twenty-first century that traditional ways of organising work may no longer be the most appropriate. Questions have been raised such as 'Why do people need to work together in a particular location?' 'Why do people need to arrive for work at a particular time and leave at a particular time?' 'Why do people need to work a certain number of continuous hours?' 'What is the best balance between home and work?' These considerations have been discussed for the past 30 plus years, and some changes have taken place over that period. By and large, however, work arrangements have not changed dramatically. The most typical changes have been flexible work hours and virtual work.

Generally, *flexible hours*, mean that employees arrive at different times and leave at different times, but all employees are at the workplace for a defined number of hours. A typical flexible schedule might mean that employees can arrive between 6 and 10 am, and can leave between 2 and 6 pm, with each employee required to be at work for 8 hours, taking time off for breaks and a meal. For example, if employees arrive at 7 am they will leave at 3 pm. The advantage is that employees have flexibility to schedule their time around family and other outside requirements, and do not need to take time off for things such as medical appointments. At the same time, all employees are together for a core period of the day (in this example 10 am to 2 pm) allowing for meetings and time spent working with others. In addition, this approach cuts down on 'rush hour' traffic congestion and parking problems caused when virtually all employees arrive at work at the same time.

Virtual work (also referred to as remote work) refers to work that does not take place in a workplace and can essentially be done from anywhere. Usually, it is associated with working from home. The number of employees working from home has increased steadily in the twenty-first century, and technology developments have made this approach increasingly attractive. In the past, it was often limited to jobs where people worked on their own and where 'outputs' could be identified relatively easily. Call centres have used virtual work because employees/service providers work over the telephone and online and are expected to complete a certain number of calls. The employee's start/end time, breaks and mealtimes are specified and monitored by the employer, calls can be recorded and listened to for quality, and outputs in terms of calls completed, sales made and so on, are observable and measurable. This does not give employees the same flexibility as flexitime but avoids the need for commuting and the employer avoids some of the costs associated with maintaining offices.

The COVID-19 pandemic changed organisation's approach to virtual work. It seems likely that these workplace effects will be widespread and long-term. The pandemic has resulted in many employees working from home, as a necessity. Consequently, both the benefits and challenges have become clearer. From the employer's perspective, if people can work effectively from home, it eliminates some need for office space and reduces costs. From the employee's perspective it increases flexibility and the need for time spent commuting. On the other hand, some managers find it difficult to monitor employees working at home, because they cannot see what the employee is doing; some employees find it difficult to be productive without the structure of the workplace and a clear distinction between work and home. Research is being done on effective management and performance in a virtual work world, but there is much to learn.

For now, we can say: Managers need to focus on objective measures of performance, rather than attempting to monitor employees' behaviour. If desired output is a certain number of 'pieces' then these can be counted, if time spent with clients this can be documented, if customer satisfaction this can be measured. For example, in academia, 'good performance' is often partly equated with research/publications. This can be objectively measured by the number and size of grants received, the number and quality of published books, journal articles and so on; the number of citations, invitations to speak and the like. It does not matter how much time the academic spends at her/his desk or computer, what matters is what s/he accomplishes. If an academic plays tennis and consequently is able to develop a mathematical equation, this is more important than if s/he sat at a computer and felt frustrated. Research has long recommended this approach, but management has sometimes remained committed to the idea that 'if I can't see you working, I don't know if you *are* working'. The pandemic may be giving us the opportunity to change this paradigm.

This may be an opportunity for employers and managers in Africa to rethink management approaches. Many African industries are built around structured work arrangements, but are these necessary? In agriculture, for example, do all workers need to start and finish at the same time? The same in mining, forestry and so on. Can some work be done at home, even if it is necessary to be at a particular workplace for parts of the day/week? For example, many jobs require substantial paperwork in addition to physical work. This is an opportunity for management to consider alternative work arrangements that may be more effective both for employees and employers. We suggest that employers conduct a job analysis of the various jobs that exist within a company, with the objective of identifying potential alternative work arrangements. These can be implemented for some employees and the results monitored, with the goal to implement more fully once the results are positive.

Work arrangements have a substantial impact on many other aspects outside of work, and work-life balance is discussed next.

Work-Life Balance

This refers to the balance we achieve between the time we devote to work versus non-work activities, and the degree to which home issues spill into the workplace and vice versa. For example, taking work home can be stressful when an employee must attend to family duties such as helping a child with homework or helping with home chores. We suggest that an appropriate balance be struck between work and life. Managers can assist employees by avoiding after-hours requests and encouraging sports and other activities. This balance will be reflected in greater productivity and satisfaction.

Job Satisfaction

An important aspect of any job is how satisfied a person is at work. We can think of satisfaction as having positive feelings about the job. Satisfaction has been related to an array of factors, including performance, attendance, turnover, loyalty/commitment and public relations. A satisfied employee is likely to feel good about the employer and company and s/he will work productively, come to work on time, want to stay with the company, be dedicated, feel a psychological bond with the company/organisation and be a good spokesperson for its products/services. These benefits mean it is important for management to find ways to ensure employee satisfaction. Dissatisfied employees can cause serious problems; from negative comments regarding the company and its products/services to work stoppages/

strikes or damage to company property. The main causes of job satisfaction/dissatisfaction are:

Fairness – all employees want to feel that they are treated fairly and if they feel that the workplace is unfair, they will be dissatisfied. Fairness applies to many aspects of work; for example:
- Pay/benefits are fair if adequate for employee's needs, comparable to other companies and industries, reflecting the type of work that is done, appropriate to levels of responsibility and authority and so on.
- Allocation of work is fair if employees are asked to do work that is consistent with job descriptions and seen as appropriate relative to others at a similar level and in similar jobs.
- Supervision/management is fair if it is supportive of subordinates' needs; neither too close or too loose, and when supervisors/managers treat employees in a way that seems justified; giving rewards and imposing sanctions equally to all employees.

Working Conditions – all employees want to work in an environment that is as safe and pleasant as possible. If the workplace is unnecessarily dirty, ugly, hazardous and so on, employees will be dissatisfied. If employees are asked to perform tasks that they believe are unsafe or behave in ways they consider unethical, they will be dissatisfied.

Co-workers – all employees desire to get on well with others at work. If co-workers are unpleasant, or if there are bullies in the workplace, employees will be dissatisfied. Group/team work forms a large part of many jobs and being able to interact positively with others in the group/team contributes to satisfaction.

The Job – all employees want to feel good about the job they do. They want to feel the job has some value and that they can be pleased when they do a good job. They want others, their superiors, co-workers, subordinates to appreciate the work they do. If employees are concerned that there is something wrong about the job itself and that others have negative feelings about it, they will be dissatisfied.

Employers/managers can pay attention to all these aspects of jobs and find ways to address causes of dissatisfaction and ensure satisfaction. In African countries, the same general categories are likely to apply but they may play out differently in terms of what specifics cause dis/satisfaction. For example, in terms of 'fairness', in the West this generally means treating everyone equally. In some African situations, it may be expected that certain people will receive preferential treatment, and this may not result in dissatisfaction (concepts of equity are discussed in the chapter on motivation). In terms of job conditions, different standards may apply in different places and what is considered 'good' may be seen as 'bad' elsewhere, depending on what is considered 'normal'. In terms of co-workers, friendliness and substantial interaction may be expected in some places, while quiet and isolation are preferred elsewhere. Finally, some types of jobs seen as desirable in one place can be undesirable in another. To assess the causes of job dis/satisfaction, it is necessary to be familiar with what is considered normal, acceptable, desirable and to adjust jobs in light of this. This is particularly important because these factors are culturally conditioned.

Many companies carry out regular 'job satisfaction' surveys to identify overall levels of satisfaction and specific areas where improvements are needed. This is a good idea for larger companies but may be difficult in smaller companies, of which there are many in Africa. These surveys require that responses be anonymous, and this is difficult in small groups. Most satisfaction surveys have been developed in the West; and may not be entirely appropriate in the African context – they may need to be adjusted and tested for that environment. Some companies, even small ones, have outside consultants who do satisfaction surveys/interviews so that employees feel comfortable responding honestly, particularly if their responses are negative. Even in very small companies, a member of the community can take on this role and provide valuable information for owners/managers.

Organisation Citizenship and Counterproductive Behaviours

Organisation citizenship behaviours (OCBs) are voluntary behaviours that foster performance and effective functioning of organisations. They are not directly required/recognised by the formal systems. For example, a long-time employee may take the time to show a new employee where the lunchroom is and how to use the facilities. This is not part of any job description or reward system but is done because it seems the right thing to do. These citizenship behaviours are outside of formal definitions but they are important to effective functioning. Managers need to find ways to acknowledge these behaviours and to encourage them. This can be as simple as saying 'thanks for showing X around the lunchroom'. The previous discussion of job satisfaction is also related to OCBs, with those who are more satisfied engaging in OCBs. A recent example of OCB concerns employees who have taken pay cuts to weather the economic downturn associated with COVID-19, including at private universities in Africa.

In contrast to OCBs, employees may engage in counterproductive work behaviours (CWBs). CWBs are also outside of job descriptions and normal sanctions. These CWBs harm the organisation or people working there. Examples include harassment and bullying, internet loafing, petty theft and negative comments. For example, one employee may continually 'tease' another about her/his social life, or disparage co-workers for not staying late at work; an employee may spend work time surfing non-work internet sites; an employee may take home office supplies; an employee may tell friends that the company is terrible to work for and the products/services are no good. All such activities harm the company and must be addressed. CWBs are a challenge for management because they are often not covered by company policies. Once identified, policies need to be developed identifying what is not acceptable. Managers should also be vigilant to detect such behaviours and take action to correct them before they impair the organisation's performance.

Conclusion

People spend a considerable part of their lives at work and thus work has a major impact on people. People are also a critical resource for organisations and contribute to effectiveness and success. We discussed how jobs can be designed to encourage motivation, satisfaction, performance and commitment, and to avoid negative health outcomes, physical and mental. Work also has an effect on life outside of work, and achieving a good work-life balance is beneficial for the employee and employer. Ensuring the workplace is safe and supportive is one of the major challenges for managers. Management needs to consider this carefully and find ways to improve the workplace wherever possible. Alternative work arrangements are one possibility, and changing technology as well as experience gained through the pandemic are contributing to changes in how management and work takes place, providing benefits and challenges for managers to make the most of the 'new world of work'.

Review/Discussion

1 Identify a job in your organisation or the University and prepare a job description for this job. You will need to observe the person doing the job, and interview them and their supervisor.
2 Consider a job that you have worked at and briefly describe the tasks involved in the doing the job. Discuss the aspects of the job that made you dis/satisfied and de/motivated. Discuss how your experience relates to the job characteristics model.
3 Using your current employment or University workload, discuss the aspects that you find stressful and how you deal with the stress. What is positive/negative about the stress?
4 At work, or University, identify OCBs or CWBs you have observed and discuss how they were handled.
5 With a small group of students, discuss your experiences of work-life challenges (work can be University requirements). Do you feel that you have adequate time for your personal life?
6 Select a job that you are familiar with and consider how alternative work arrangements could apply to this job. Would you personally like to work flexibly or virtually? Discuss why/why not.

Exercise: Bafia Dance – A Metaphor
for Cameroon and Africa

Thanks to: Vincent Bagire (Makerere University, Uganda), Gladys Nyamagere (Ardhi University, Tanzania) and Simon Sigue (Athabasca University, Canada).

The Bafia tribe of Cameroon is in the central part of the country, predominantly in the tropical savanna and forest. Their territory cuts across these two climatic conditions. They include both Muslims and Christians. They are culturally known for the Bafia dance.

The Bafia dance is one of the most popular traditional dances in Cameroon, used at many functions ranging from rituals, political rallies, diplomacy, entertainment and national welcome. It is a group dance with men and women dancing to a rhythm, accompanied by drums and other traditional instruments. The key characteristic that underlies this metaphor is that movements consist of one step ahead and two steps back. The dancers move ahead as well as backward. The dance is a fitness exercise, requiring mental alertness and psychological cohesion with dance mates. The dance involves training and skill building to have harmonious rhythms.

Culturally the dance represents the beliefs and practices of happiness, togetherness and enjoyment. It is a show of cultural pride, with no hurry by individuals to move on or leave others behind.

From a Business/Management perspective, the Bafia dance provides positive and negative lessons. Positively, it teaches managers to be different, to look ahead and pursue goals with clear leadership, step by step ahead; not crowd movements that do not direct steps. In business/management, leadership is critical; someone is expected to inspire, guide and direct the actions of others towards defined goals. The Bafia is a signal for team-work, no one dances alone, they form a team, train together so as to work together.

On the other hand, The Bafia dance may suggest that expectations will be not be met, and energies to pursue goals fall apart as they step backwards; this may illustrate a lack of goal management, not moving steadily ahead, a lack of consistency, not progressive but rather retrogressive, losing focus on the goal ahead. More positively, the backwards steps could also be interpreted to mean a period of reflection, a time for consideration, the opportunity for feedback and a move to ensure that no one is left behind.

We conclude that the Bafia dance, by nature of those patterns has important messages. We appreciate that while negatives may be discerned, the purpose of the dance is the configuration created. This is how managers must be focused, clear on their objectives to create value and achieve worthwhile outputs.

Assignment

1 Identify and watch a Bafia dance video in a group (three or four students). There are many variations so you may want to watch more than one. Identify characteristics of the dance that you feel help understand the culture of Cameroon.

2 Identify and discuss how the Bafia dance can be related positively to decision making for managers and leaders. Identify the weakness illustrated by the Bafia dance that may be common among managers and leaders.

3 Identify and discuss environmental factors that may make managers fall into 'Bafia dancing', i.e., moving ahead and backwards.

4 As a student of business/management, how would you advise contemporary managers and leaders to maintain the message of the Bafia dance but progress towards the set goals.

5 Identify and discuss the management and leadership style that the Bafia dance describes.

References

Hackman, J. R., & Oldham, G. R. (1976). "Motivation through the design of work: Test of a theory". *Organizational Behavior and Human Performance*, *16*(2), 250–279.

4   Motivation

Learning Outcomes

After completing this chapter, you will be able to:

- Explain the meaning of motivation and how motivation may differ from one location to another
- Outline the major theories of motivation, and illustrate how and why these might or might not work in various locations, including African countries
- Discuss the importance of motivation to behaviour, and explain the challenges of understanding motivation, particularly in unfamiliar locations and among different groups
- Give examples of how behaviour is linked to motivation
- Identify and discuss how African characteristics may be linked to motivation

Thought Starters

The women at work sat around a table, busily embroidering children's dresses. They talked constantly about their children, their husbands, the food they would cook later, what the neighbour had done …. The room was noisy and busy. My reaction was "how can they get anything done in this environment? Maybe if each woman had her own table, they would be more productive?" I soon learned that I was wrong. It was the social setting that motivated these women and without this environment, production decreased.

Summary

This chapter summarises what we mean by motivation and why understanding the consequences of motivation is critical to effective management and organisational performance/success. It looks at major

DOI: 10.4324/9781003036838-4

theories of motivation developed in the West, including needs, equity, rewards/reinforcement, goals, expectations and delegation/partici-pation. It examines their transferability to the African context and relates this to desirable managerial approaches. We discuss the ques-tion, *Is motivation universal or culture bound?* and offer some insights to guide management in Africa.

Introduction

Motivation refers to inner urges that cause people to behave in certain ways. At work, people are highly motivated when they work hard to accomplish objectives that are consistent with the organisation's goals, de-motivated when they seem disinterested and need to be pushed to perform. We observe behaviour, not its cause(s), i.e. motivation. What makes people motivated/de-motivated is complex and can be caused by psychological, demographic and work-related factors.

It is inaccurate to say people are de-motivated. People are moti-vated in some direction; the question is the direction. Someone de-motivated at work, is motivated in some non-work direction; i.e., they would rather be doing something other than work. The termi-nology of de-motivation is used frequently in everyday language, so it will be used in this chapter. When someone is de-motivated, their performance is less than expected, therefore motivation is of great interest to managers. Success and profitability are related to people's performance/productivity, and managers want to ensure employees perform at a high level.

Within our own culture, we try to draw meaningful conclusions about the causes of motivation because we share certain basic val-ues, attitudes and beliefs. If a co-worker suddenly seems de-mo-tivated, I might consider recent events and think, "Oh, she was passed over for that promotion she thought she deserved, that's probably why". I am drawing on my own feelings, and a general belief that when we think we have been treated unfairly (or inequi-tably) it is de-motivating. I may be right in my attribution regarding my co-worker, or I may be wrong (she might have problems at home of which I am unaware that affect her work behaviour), but I do have a basis on which to hypothesize – her behaviour tells me something is not right, and I use my own experience to find a reason. Because behaviour is caused by inner urges, however, I cannot be sure of my attribution. We cannot even be sure ourselves of what motivates us, and one hears people say things like "I don't know why I feel de-motivated".

Imagine how difficult it is to understand motivation in unfamiliar locations. For example, some African groups believe rewards should be allocated according to need rather than performance – a person with several dependents should receive more pay than someone with none, even though the person with none works harder and performs better. An American manager would reward the high performer and expect this to be motivating. In the African circumstance, this could be seen as inequitable and de-motivate both parties. It would be difficult for the American manager to understand the causes of motivation/de-motivation in this situation.

This chapter explores a series of motivation theories, largely developed and tested in North America, and asks "To what extent are these valid in the African context?" and "What would affect their relevance in Africa?"

Theories of Motivation

The major theories of motivation encompass needs, equity, expectations, rewards, goals and delegation/participation. Each is explained briefly then considered from African perspectives. The links between African factors and motivation are conceptual rather than empirical, but we draw on research where possible.

Needs

People have certain needs and behaviours are intended to fulfil these needs – we act to meet our needs. If you need food (are hungry), you will try to satisfy this need (in New York City, they might look for a restaurant). Behaviour (looking for a restaurant) thus reflects the need (hunger).

Maslow's Hierarchy

The best-known theory is Maslow's (1954) *hierarchy of needs*. Maslow proposed a hierarchy of five levels – going from most basic needs (1) at the bottom to the highest-level (5) at the top:

1 Physiological needs concern survival, the need for food, water, shelter and sex.
2 Security needs concern continued survival, assurance of the availability of food, water, shelter and sex in the future.

3 Social needs concern interactions/communication with others, friendships and relationships.
4 Esteem needs concern feeling positive about oneself, praise, recognition and self-esteem.
5 Self-actualisation concerns being the best one can be, doing things that are important and accomplishing difficult goals.

Maslow proposed that each level became important, and a motivating force, only when the previous level had been satisfied. The basic, physiological needs were paramount until satisfied; once fulfilled, you focus on security. Once security was achieved, social needs come to the fore. Once social needs were met, esteem becomes important, and when other needs were met, self-actualisation is the main motivating force.

The needs move from concrete to abstract. Survival needs are well defined for all – everybody needs a meal and medication when sick, etc. The highest level, self-actualisation is unclear and varies from person to person (one person aspiring to being company CEO, making a billion dollars a year; another choosing to be an ascetic and lead a monk's spiritual life). Basic physiological and security needs are essentially universal – people everywhere share these and they will be the dominant motivational forces until satisfied. People without enough to eat, whether they are in Australia or Zimbabwe, will be motivated primarily by the need to find food and behave accordingly.

Empirical studies of Maslow's hierarchy in countries around the world suggest that a hierarchy of needs is universal, but that the order of the hierarchy varies. Higher order needs are more culturally/ nationally contingent. Even the most basic needs vary culturally – in Canada, the foods chosen may be different from those in Cameroon, certain foods may be prohibited, cooking methods prescribed and so on. These differences may be related to other needs; for example, religious customs often dictate what, how and when we eat.

The order of needs may vary. Social needs can be most important for cultural reasons, or geography determine the importance of security, in locations subject to natural disasters. The expression of needs and how they are satisfied varies; for example, many cultures have rules regarding sex, often tied to religious beliefs, and culture influences how people meet their social needs and what is meant by esteem or self-actualisation. Other national characteristics may affect needs – in communist countries, basic needs are provided by the government and they can be taken for granted; self-actualisation may be contrary to certain religious beliefs because God is the only one who is able to determine one's fate.

Managers can use the concept of needs to help motivate employees, but to be effective they need to understand which needs are most important and how a person or group prefers to satisfy them. For example, with employees of different age groups, the approaches to motivating each age group may vary. In North America, Maslow's hierarchy illustrates the need to give employees opportunities to meet higher-level needs on the job. Providing opportunities for social, esteem and self-actualisation is seen as motivating, while lower-level needs are assumed to have been met. In African countries, if poverty and disease are prevalent and social security systems are limited, with employees living on minimal wages, basic needs may not be met and providing breakfast/lunch on the job could be more motivating than added responsibility, praise or making a job more intrinsically interesting.

McClelland: Achievement, Affiliation, Power

McClelland's (1967) theory suggested that different needs manifest themselves more or less in different people. Need for achievement, affiliation and power have been considered most relevant in organisations. These have been investigated cross-culturally, and there is some evidence that they may all be important, but there is also reason to question this, and some have argued that the achievement construct may be peculiar to the English language. One study comparing China with North America found that Chinese respondents scored uniformly lower on all the needs measured. The best explanation was that more important needs from a Chinese perspective were not being captured in the North American framework. North American-based theory may exclude needs that are important in other locations, such as African countries.

High need for achievement means someone has a drive and is motivated to do tasks that are difficult and accomplish objectives seen as worthwhile. What is difficult in one location may be somewhat easy in another, and what is considered worthwhile can vary. If we accept that some people everywhere exhibit a need for achievement, the expression of this need may differ – some people value autonomy and will seek to achieve goals on their own, for others, structure is valued, and people seek to achieve what their superiors deem important. Historical and geographic factors play a role in how needs are exhibited and satisfied. Achievement can come by rising in a bureaucracy (perpetuated from colonial systems) or the achievement of working independently on a small farm.

The existence of manifest needs is likely universal – some needs will be more important to some people and will be manifested in their behaviour. Managers must understand which needs are most relevant for their employees. Using manifest needs to motivate people is a valid strategy around the world but figuring out which needs are manifest and how they can be best satisfied requires substantial sensitivity given the diversity of people.

Herzberg's Two Factor Theory

Herzberg's theory and subsequent work on intrinsic and extrinsic motivational factors, as well as job design, followed from earlier need theories. Herzberg (1959) argued that there are two sets of factors associated with any job and with a person's motivation relative to the job. One set is intrinsic to the job itself – how interesting, challenging, rewarding the job is – and these factors motivate. The second set is extrinsic to the job – physical conditions, money, supervision, co-workers and so on – these need to be met for a person to be satisfied, but do not actually motivate. The absence of extrinsic factors can, however, de-motivate. These concepts appeal because they separate what makes us want to do a job from the conditions in which work and separate satisfaction from motivation – being satisfied with working conditions does not mean you will be motivated to work hard and perform well. Herzberg's theory resulted in a focus on designing jobs to be intrinsically motivating. Such jobs incorporated variety, autonomy, feedback and task significance.

The distinction between intrinsic and extrinsic job aspects may be universal, but have different roles to play in motivation. The relationship to motivation is not necessarily the same around the world; however, extrinsic factors essentially relate to the lower-order needs and intrinsic factors to higher-order ones. In poorer countries the extrinsic factors are often valued as motivators as much as or more than intrinsic ones. Workers in these countries may want jobs with little variety and autonomy, and speak of the importance of pay, supervision, working conditions and other extrinsic factors. In one study, employees were asked why they continued to work with the firm. They responded that they could do their task well, with little thought, while conversing with co-worker friends, their supervisor helped them do their jobs, and the factory was clean. Asked if rotating jobs would make the work more interesting, they said they preferred to do the job they already knew well. When asked if each person should check her/his own quality, they responded that the people assigned to do quality checking knew that aspect and should continue to do their specialised job. Variety and autonomy were seen as inefficient and would likely have been de-motivating. Job significance did provide a potential motivating tool; employees were most interested to know, and see physical evidence, that the electronic parts they made were used in computers. This scenario is likely the reality of many jobs in African countries, where extrinsic factors may play an important role in motivation.

The relationship between satisfaction and motivation can also differ from place to place. In some locations a satisfied employee will feel an obligation to work hard and perform well. In other places, it is possible that being satisfied results in a relaxed attitude and affects performance negatively. In contrast, if employees are dissatisfied, they might be motivated to work hard, feeling that if they performed well, they could change the situation, hard work could take one's mind off dissatisfaction and so on. There are many potential relationships, and, again, the effective manager needs to consider the relationships in her/his organisation and culture.

Equity

Equity theory proposes that individuals consider what they put into a given situation (inputs) relative to what they get out of the situation (outcomes) and compares this ratio with the inputs/outcomes of some other(s). If the relationships are judged fair/equitable, the person will seek to maintain the current situation. If seen as unfair/inequitable, the person will seek to change the situation in the future. For example:

If a student works hard, attends classes, hands in assignments (inputs) and gets a grade of 'B' (outcome), she will then compare this input–output ratio to that of others in the class. If the comparison seems fair, she will continue to work hard. If others have done little work but ended up with higher marks, the comparison will seem unfair. The student will try to change some of the inputs or outcomes. It is difficult to change other people's inputs/outcomes, so it is most likely the student will try to change her own inputs/outcomes. The student may ask the professor for a better grade (outcome), but if that does not work, the student may lower her inputs in the future. The impact of a perception of inequity is de-motivating.

Equity stresses the importance of evaluating and rewarding people fairly, so that good work is rewarded equitably; however, what is considered equitable may vary. An earlier example talked of a group in Africa that believes *need* should be rewarded over *performance*. This seems inequitable in North American. In the student example, if the professor only gave A's to those from a certain social class this would be considered unfair in North America, but elsewhere, where society respects and values a class system, this could be acceptable. Managers need to understand what are considered inputs and what outcomes are valued, to use equity to motivate employees. In a location where the number of dependents is believed to entitle someone to greater rewards, the number of dependents could be considered a valid input; where age is accepted as giving rights to certain rewards, this may be a normal input. In some places, men and women doing the same work are paid differentially because women are deemed to be less valuable than men, or because it is believed they need less compensation. Discrimination based on factors such as gender, age, race, religion, language, physical ability and sexual preference is unlawful in some countries but accepted in others. We do not advocate such discrimination and would want to change it, but we do recognise its existence.

Rewards-Reinforcement

Equity theory incorporates rewards as a means for motivating employees. Reinforcement theory ties rewards to behaviour directly as a means of encouraging desired behaviour and discouraging/eliminating undesired behaviour. The idea of reinforcing desired behaviour through rewards is that people repeat behaviours that are rewarded, and behaviour that is not rewarded eventually disappears. People use reinforcement often; parents promise children ice cream when they finish their homework (and withhold the ice cream if not completed); pet owners give dogs treats when they obey commands (and withhold when they do not). Reinforcement does not necessarily incorporate equity and to encourage a person to change behaviour, one might reward them in what seems an inequitable manner. Reinforcement theory generally avoids punishment, as punishment is believed to have undesired side effects.

Encouraging desired behaviour through rewards is probably effective in a variety of locations. Rewards must be desired to be motivating, and this means that they should provide a means to satisfy needs. Reinforcement is culturally contingent in terms of understanding which rewards will be most effective, when to give rewards, how to give them and so on.

Consider *what* we use as rewards:

- In North America, money is considered a valued reward, and increased compensation is used to motivate employees who perform well. In other locations, people work until they have enough money to pay for necessities, and additional compensation means that they are likely to stop working.

* In North America, it is appropriate to single out individuals for doing a good job. In Japan and Eastern countries, singling out is used to indicate that an individual has not been performing up to standard.
* In North America, coaching, in which positive aspects of work are recognised and suggestions for improvement given, is considered a valuable approach. In India, straightforward criticism is preferred, and people expect to be told that they have made mistakes and to be sanctioned for these mistakes.

In Africa, generally money is valued as a reward, but titles are also valued. The title *Owekitibwa,* conferred by the *Kabaka* (King) of the Buganda kingdom of Uganda is seen as highly motivating. It is less common to single out people for reward/punishment because of the collectivist tendency.

Consider *when* we give rewards:

* Some societies believe in giving rewards often and as soon as desired behaviour occurs; others use rewards only occasionally. North Americans typically believe that rewards should be frequent.
* Some societies set short-term objectives and tie rewards to these; others favour long-term objectives and link rewards generally to these. North Americans typically focus on short-term, specific objectives and tie rewards to these (for example commissions).
* Some societies give small rewards; others believe in substantial ones. North Americans typically believe that rewards should be substantial.

In Africa, in most organisations, particularly public ones, rewards are given based on experience and the position held and less based on performance. This means some employees may focus on rising through the organisational hierarchy, including through means other than performance.

Consider *how* we give rewards:

* Rewards can be given to individuals or to groups. North Americans favour individual rewards. Group/team rewards are

preferred in most African countries; however, the influence of Western management practices has resulted in cases of individual rewards, which are sometimes interpreted as 'favoritism'. Managers need to find mechanisms to support team effectiveness to ensure each member contributes optimally, when the reward is for the group.

- Rewards can be given by a superior, by co-workers or by subordinates. North American rewards are usually allocated by superiors, sometimes by co-workers.
- Rewards can be given formally or informally, publicly or privately. North American rewards are given both formally and informally, almost always in public. In contrast, discipline is usually formal and done in private.

Many societies feel that punishment is an important part of motivation. Reinforcement theory focuses on rewards and incorporates the belief that people are changeable. North American reinforcement theory stresses the potential negative impact of punishment, which is suggested only as a last resort. In many societies, the prevalent belief is that if someone behaves in undesirable ways, it is because they are 'bad', and punishment/sanctions are the only way to stop undesirable behaviour.

Using reinforcement well requires a focus on the local environment to match rewards to expectations. Reinforcement can be effective, but only when rewards are appropriate from the perspective of those receiving the reinforcement. Where public criticism and discipline are the norm, managers will have to consider carefully how to administer such criticism and discipline, as it can make some managers uncomfortable, and it can have undesirable results.

Goal Setting

There is evidence that goals focus energy and improve performance. The North American literature links specific and challenging goals, once accepted, to higher outputs (Locke & Latham, 1990). Acceptance is often linked to participation in setting goals, and participatively set goals are seen as more effective than assigned goals. Goals alone stimulate productivity, but they are especially effective when linked to desired rewards.

Cross-national studies suggest goals are effective in an array of countries, including Australia, the Caribbean, Israel and Sri Lanka.

Based on this, goals may have a universal effect on performance and be useful in African countries; however, there are national and cultural factors that might affect the use of goal setting:

- A feminine society might see specific/difficult goals as encouraging competition and regard them negatively.
- A collective society would see group goals as appropriate and react negatively to individual ones.
- A society that seeks certainty might find difficult goals stressful because of fear that they could not be achieved.

Other factors could also affect how goals work:

- Postcolonial societies, such as those in Africa, may associate goal setting with colonial masters and resent them.
- People in tropical locations often have a 'casual' approach to time/life, with immediate desires/needs more important than plans, and goal accomplishment may be difficult. In this regard, the phrase "there is no hurry in Africa" has been used; however, a sense of time and deadliness has been embraced across Africa with 'time management' training interventions being implemented.
- People with a high need for achievement benefit from reaching a challenging goal, but those with a low need may see little value in reaching such a goal.
- People who feel little control over their environment, may find setting a specific target unrealistic and possibly going against God's will.
- In hierarchical societies, goals would be set by those in a position of power, where in more egalitarian societies, participative goal setting is preferable.
- People with a short-term orientation will favour immediate goals, with rewards tied closely to performance; where orientations are long term, future-oriented goals are best.

African countries are more collective/communal, want certainty, have hierarchical structures, are somewhat fatalistic and short-term oriented, and managers will want to experiment with different types of goals to determine what works well in different locations. There is evidence that the effectiveness of participation varies from culture to culture, as does the nature of appropriate feedback (Audia and Tams, 2002).

Expectations

Expectancy theory is based on an individual's expectations about the outcome of their actions. A person considers a situation and asks:

1 "If I try/work harder/put in a lot of effort will my performance improve?" (expectancy 1)
2 "If my performance improves, will my rewards increase?" (expectancy 2/instrumentality)
3 "How much do I value these rewards?" (valence)

Answers range from zero to one. If the answer is clearly no = zero; if clearly yes = one; in-between, the score is some fraction to indicate how close to 'no' or 'yes' (0.1 is close to 'no', 0.9 close to 'yes'). If the answer to any question is 'no', the person will not put in much effort. If I think increased effort will not result in increased performance, there is no reason to increase effort, if increased performance won't lead to greater rewards, or I don't value the rewards, there is no point increasing efforts. Rewards are extrinsic (pay, time off, etc.) and intrinsic (enjoy doing a good job, sense of achievement, etc.). Motivation is a multiplicative relationship; motivation = expectancy 1 × expectancy 2 × valence. The higher (closer to 1) the score, the higher a person's motivation will be, and the lower (closer to 0), the less motivation.

Using expectancy theory to motivate employees entails ensuring people feel they can perform well if they put in effort, that they have appropriate goals (linking to goal setting), that performance is rewarded fairly (linking to equity), and that rewards are valued (linking to needs and reinforcement). Expectancy is built around individual performance/rewards, rational/linear thinking and control of one's environment. The individual logically evaluates the likelihood of various outcomes and chooses on this basis whether to exert effort or not. It is based on egalitarian beliefs and the sense that individuals have options. They are not bound to do what a superior wants/expects, and can seek alternatives rather than accept a situation seen as unfair/unpleasant. Individualism, control of one's environment, and rational/linear thinking are part of the North American and 'Western' cultural context. In many parts of the world, the context is essentially the reverse: the group is more important, the world is controlled by those in positions of power or by the spirit realm, and people's thinking is circular. This is the case in many parts of Africa and the logic of expectancy theory may not transfer. Nevertheless, aspects of expectancy can be used. It is appropriate to ensure that an employee's increased

effort will result in increased performance, that performance is appropriately rewarded, and that rewards are the desired ones. The caveats
previously discussed apply – the effective manager will understand
the cultural/national context and adapt the *how* and *when* of rewards
appropriately.

Delegation/Participation

North American management literature is built around delegation and
participation as important aspects of effectiveness. Managers delegate
responsibilities to subordinates and provide subordinates with the
authority and resources to carry out these responsibilities. Employees
want to have responsibility and appreciate the trust in their abilities/
attitudes that accompanies delegation. Delegation is seen as effective
for developing employees' abilities and decision-making capabilities.
Participation in decision-making is believed essential to acceptance
of decisions and willingness to carry out decisions. Delegation and
participation go hand in hand because effective delegation relies on
employees accepting the delegated responsibility, and this acceptance
is enhanced by participation in decisions, including decisions regarding delegation. Together, delegation and participation provide a work
environment conducive to hard work, good performance and contributes to individual motivation and development.

   The universal effectiveness of delegation and participation is not
clear, and many cultures do not have a tradition of either. Rather,
the manager's job is to make decisions and the subordinate's job is
to receive instructions and carry them out. Managers are expected
to monitor subordinates closely to ensure instructions are carried
out properly, and to correct subordinates immediately if they devi-
ate. Employees from societies without a tradition of delegation/
participation believe that managers have the ability to make decisions;
that is why they are managers. Subordinates do not have these abilities
and are more comfortable with managers making decisions and giving
instructions. They are uncomfortable if asked to participate and take
on responsibility beyond the simple performance of assigned tasks.

   One legacy of colonialism in African countries seems to be a tradition of non-delegation and non-participation that makes it difficult for
managers and subordinates to accept and implement these practices.
Colonies were governed from the land of the colonial masters, delegation and participation were discouraged. People in former colonies
may continue to be reluctant to delegate/accept delegation, and may be
uncomfortable with participative practices. At the same time, where

managers want to delegate and encourage participation, and where subordinates are appropriately trained and coached, it seems to have a positive impact on motivation and performance. Managers wishing to experiment with delegation/participation, in locations where these are not the norm, need to implement these approaches cautiously and examine the results carefully. In particular, the managers should look out for situations where delegation is seen as 'setting me up to fail' by the person being delegated to.

Is Motivation Universal or Culture Bound?

There are aspects to North American theories of motivation discussed that can be applied in spite of national and cultural differences, and other aspects are affected by culture and other national characteristics. The theories appear to apply at a 'macro' level. The big picture is universal; i.e., people everywhere have needs, people seek some kind of equity, people react to rewards, they work toward goals and have expectations about performance. The details, the *how*, *what* and *when* of implementing them, are likely culturally bound and must change cross-nationally. All managers face challenges in motivating employees. Effective managers in African countries will be sensitive to the cultural/national context affecting employee motivation. Good managers will try a variety of approaches and watch results closely to find those that work best and replicate them.

Smith, Peterson, and Schwartz (2002) found nations using participative guidance sources were characterised by high individualism, autonomy, egalitarianism, low power distance and harmony, values typical in the nations of Western Europe. Nations that relied on superiors and rules were collective, high on embeddedness, hierarchy, power distance, mastery and masculinity. Many African nations are closer to this profile. The authors caution that the sources of guidance were derived from formal organisations, rather than groups such as families and family members, and these groups would likely be important in some countries. In African countries, tribes/ethnic groups may be important as well as older members of these groups.

Conclusion

In this chapter various North American motivational approaches were explored against the background of national/cultural variations and the African context. Some aspects of motivation may be universal, others are culture bound. Managers can use the broad concepts of motivation – needs, equity, expectancy and so on – as a base for understanding motivation in Africa. They will find that the details of how these concepts apply will differ from place to place and even employee to employee. Motivation is a critical aspect of management and the African context is no different in this regard. Managers everywhere need to find ways to ensure that employees work hard and perform at peak levels. Especially in today's globally competitive environment, maximum performance can give a firm a competitive edge. Taking the time and making the effort to understand motivation is central to effective management.

Review/Discussion

1   Select a motivational theory to investigate. Explain, from your personal perspective, how you have experienced motivation and how your experience fits or does not fit with the theory. Meet with a colleague from another culture and explain your experience and get their reaction. Discuss how your perceptions are similar or different.

2   Develop a cultural value profile for an African country. Imagine that you are going to that country as a manager. Discuss how you will approach your subordinates in the country to ensure that they are well motivated and perform at a high level.

Exercise: Differing Views of Motivation

A Canadian consultant was engaged to carry out a series of training programs in India for academics that wished to be able to undertake management consulting assignments. The program was built around a series of practice assignments. Participants had to write proposals, do mock interviews with clients, playing the parts of both consultant and client, and carry out assignments, as well as preparing reports. The programs were generally well received. The Canadian normally focused his comments on how participants could improve performance. The Canadian was concerned with ensuring that the participants felt good about their experience in the training sessions and believed that focusing on improvement was the best approach. Some Indian participants expressed a wish that he focus on what they had done wrong and some said they needed harsher discipline. Some of the participants believed that more direct criticism of their performance would better help them improve. To some extent, the Canadian style can be seen as reflecting a *participative* approach, while the participants were expecting a more *autocratic* approach. The Canadian focused on rewarding good behaviour, while the Indians wanted more focus on punishment.

Assignment

1 As the Canadian consultant, how would you deal with this situation?
2 How would you motivate your participants?
3 How would you expect African participants to react to the Canadian's approach?

References

Audia, P. G., & Tams, S. (2002). Goal setting, performance appraisal, and feedback across cultures. In M. J. Gannon & K. L. Newman (Eds.), *The Blackwell handbook of cross-cultural management* (pp. 142–154). Oxford: Blackwell Publishers.

Herzberg, F. (1959). *The motivation to work*. New York, NY: John Wiley.

Locke, E. A., & Latham, G. P. (1990). *A theory of goal setting and task performance*. Englewood Cliffs, NJ: Prentice Hall.

Maslow, A. H. (1954). *Motivation and personality*. New York, NY: Harper.

McClelland, D. C. (1967). *The achieving society*. New York, NY: Free Press.

Smith, P. B., Peterson, M. F., & Schwartz, S. (2002). "Cultural values, sources of guidance and their relevance to managerial behavior". *Journal of Cross Cultural Psychology*, *32*(2), 188–208.

5 Decision-Making and Communication

Learning Outcomes

After completing this chapter, you will be able to:

- Explain decision-making theories and various types of decisions
- Describe the decision-making process and biases in decision-making
- Define communication and illustrate with a model
- Compare and contrast verbal and non-verbal communication
- Understand and apply effective interpersonal communications
- Discuss effective upward/downward/lateral communication
- Identify and describe barriers to effective communications
- Discuss language and cultural issues relevant to communication in the African context

Thought Starters

Winjo wach loyo bor im gi chwe – Heeding counsel is better than a ram's fat tail (Proverb).

A group of blind people heard that a strange animal, an elephant, was in the town. They said, "We must touch it to see what it is like". One touched the trunk and said, "it is like a thick snake", another touched its ear and thought it was like a kind of fan. A third felt its leg and decided it was like a pillar or a tree trunk. The one who touched its side said, "it is a wall". Another felt its tail and described it as "a rope" and the last felt its tusk and thought it was like a spear. How can they decide what an elephant is like?

Summary

This chapter explains decision-making theories, various types of decisions and describes the decision-making process and its biases. We also examine communication, outlining a model including verbal and

DOI: 10.4324/9781003036838-5

non-verbal communication. Interpersonal communications, upward/downward/lateral networks and the grapevine are presented, followed by barriers to effective communications – filtering, perceptions, information overload, the internet, emotions and silence. The chapter concludes with a description language and cultural issues relevant to communication in the African context.

Introduction

We can ask why decisions should be made and what role theory plays in understanding effective decision-making. Everybody makes many decisions – from simple (to watch a football match or read an article) to more complex (take a professional development course, invest in the stock exchange or start a business). The essence of decision-making is evaluation of alternatives to choose the most appropriate one. In business context, managers/leaders are faced with demands to make decisions in increasingly competitive environments. They must decide what markets to enter, what products/services to offer, what customers to target, who to hire or fire, where to get financing, etc. These require sensitivity to context, attention to content and presentation of information and even the use of intuition (Turpin & Marais, 2004). Some tools to aid in decision-making include decision support technology, and self-help tools such as office software.

Sound decisions are based on evidence and poor ones can lead to misallocation of scarce resources, poor performance and dissatisfaction of stakeholders. At worst, a manager may be relieved of her/his job because of poor performance arising from their decisions. Building the capacity for effective decision-making is critical, and is intended, where possible, to remove guesswork by following a scientific approach, grounded in theory. Decisions in organisations should not be made as if it is a lottery; they should be carefully thought out.

Decision-Making Theories

Two common approaches to decision-making are rational/normative (Simon, 1977) and behavioural (Cyert & March, 1963).

Bounded rationality (Simon, 1977) suggests that decisions are as good as the information accessed during the analysis of a situation and should change as new evidence becomes available. Simon refers to 'satisficing' (combining 'satisfy' and 'suffice') where decisions satisfy minimum requirements rather than seeking the best ones. Decisions are also constrained by 'cognitive limits' of decision makers because managers may not have the insights or conceptual and analytical capacity to assess circumstances and use the information generated to make decisions.

Rational Decision-Making

This approach focuses on making decisions to maximise/optimise organisational efficiency and effectiveness. The underlying assumptions include:

*   Availability of perfect information and certainty of the environment
*   Maximising behaviour, seeking an optimal solution
*   Consensus on organisational values shared by members
*   Analytical sophistication of decision makers, including the ability to rigorously analyse data to provide information to guide decision-making.

This approach begins by clearly defining the decision to be made and the objectives to be achieved. Based on this, relevant information is gathered. This is followed by an analysis of the situation in terms of what courses of action are available and how the data may be interpreted. This leads to developing different alternatives which can be evaluated, based on pre-determined criteria, in terms of outcomes. Alternatives are compared to determine which best achieves desired objectives, and the preferred alternative is assessed in terms of benefits and drawbacks. Finally, the decision is implemented and outcomes monitored and assessed.

   This approach is logical and attractive; however, it has limitations. The assumption of perfect information often does not hold, and most decisions are made in uncertain environments. It can include complex mathematical techniques such as linear programming or game theory that are unfamiliar to many managers and may have limited application in real-life situations. Decisions are often made within a limited time frame and with limited resources which constrains the use of rational decision-making. The assumption of 'consensus on values' overlooks conflicts among individuals and groups about objectives, priorities and the best strategies to pursue.

Four Types of Rationality

Simon asked *on what objectives, and whose values, should rationality be judged?* He identified:

1 'Objectively' rational, if maximising for known values in each situation.
2 'Subjectively' rational, if maximising attainment of given values in the context of the 'bounded' or limited knowledge of the decision maker (i.e., bounded rationality).
3 'Organisationally' rational, if oriented to attainment of organisational goals/objectives.
4 'Personally' rational, if oriented to an individual's goals.

Cyert and March (1963) emphasised the 'political' process involved in the reconciliation of goals, saying that organisations do not have objectives, only people do. Organisational objectives are the end product of complex and continuous interactions between individuals and groups within and outside the organisation.

Behavioural Decision-Making

This approach is linked to the behaviour of individuals based on psychology, sociology and anthropology. Behavioural theories are concerned with *how managers actually make decisions* not *how managers should make decisions.*

Studies show that multiple goals in organisations may be in conflict and need to be reconciled in decision-making so the most appropriate/optimal is adopted. Coalitions exist and organisations can be a set of competing interests. These factors affect how decisions are made in reality – with trade-offs and compromises rather than optimisation. Groups with conflicting interest include shareholders, customers, creditors, civil society, suppliers, employees, etc. Considering the allocation of surpluses, shareholders may see the optimal decision as increases in dividends while employees see it as an increase in wages; the real-life decision may be a smaller increase in both. Similarly, different production, inventory, profit, sales goals result in trade-offs.

When resources are scarce decisions about their allocation are often more political than rational and preceded by working behind the scenes, using social networks, and building coalitions around preferred outcomes. Rational allocation of scarce resources is desirable, with all alternatives considered, but this is not always the reality.

Political decision-making is based on who is more astute in building coalitions and influencing others rather than on a rational evaluation.

African Decision Preferences

We have not identified literature on how these theories apply in the African context and there is a need to explore their applicability and test their efficacy in this context. One study of six decision makers in South Africa showed that politicians make decisions that favour their own position, rather than aiming at decisions good for the wider society; and that one needs to consider what a manager is thinking (Turpin & Marais, 2004). This reflects a behavioural approach and anecdotal evidence suggests that most organisational decisions are behavioural, based on consensus, rather than strictly rational, particularly in small and family-owned business. *Rational* and *behavioural* are two ends of a continuum, and real-life decisions occur between these two extremes and are in effect a combination, and this is likely the case in the African context.

Okonedo (2018) says that decisions are based on national culture (and sub-cultures) including customs, traditions, beliefs, taboos, faith, institutions, personality and psychological behaviours that distinguish decision makers based on age, experience and level of education. In Africa, the process is somewhat logical, time based and systematic with the aim of choosing one alternative from several; however, there are trade-offs between rational and behavioural, tilting towards behavioural. Our observation is that decisions in Africa are loosely based on logic and time constraints typical in the West, but time is more flexible and consensus considered desirable. Rational decision-making may be 'logical'; however, decisions derive external validity from social norms, and are thus made in a cultural context. In African organisations, decisions are often top-down, although participatory approaches, where subordinates provide input, are increasingly being encouraged and adopted.

The hierarchy needs to be considered due to patriarchal cultures, and relatively high power distance, of most African societies. Top-down decisions were also typical in colonial times and persist in many former colonies. Decisions at lower levels may be needed for timeliness and urgency, but may await a nod from higher authorities. Bureaucracy is also common, and the vision and desired results are decided by top management and communicated to those at lower management. While these descriptions are true in many African countries, the communal nature of the culture provides opportunities for more consultation and participation, and managers may find these approaches can be successful if implemented with appropriate mentoring and training.

Types of Decisions

In organisations, decisions are made at three levels, operational, tactical and strategic, and the characteristics of decisions at each level differ. Operational decisions are predominantly repetitive on a daily/weekly basis (how many widgets to make in a week based on sales forecasts). They are characterised by a few uncertainties. Tactical decisions have some uncertainty and are made from time to time, at short intervals (to shut down a widget line for repairs). Strategic decisions are essentially one time and unique, with long-term implications (to change from making widgets to making swidgets). Strategic decisions are the most uncertain because of the longer time horizon and broader scope in a changing and unpredictable environment.

Being clear about which decisions should be made at what level and by whom is necessary for coherence and effectiveness. Operational decisions are made by lower-level managers in close touch with the situation that requires decision and action – the decision maker physically sees the problems that need attention. Tactical decisions are required because of an inspection or performance audit that draws the attention of the decision maker to a situation requiring action. Strategic decisions are concerned with the overall direction of the organisation and are based on a comprehensive analysis of the external and internal environments and consideration of many alternatives.

Decisions can be classified as *programmed* (well-structured, repetitive and handled by routine rules/procedures), usually dominant at lower/middle organisational levels and likely operational and tactical, and *non-programmed* (unstructured, unique) requiring imagination, initiative, complex analyses and predominantly encountered at upper levels and are strategic. Decision makers draw from specific disciplines depending on the nature of the decision to be made. For employee motivation, theories of motivation found in psychology and sociology are more relevant than theories in economics, while for new market decisions, various economic models/theories are relevant.

Decisions are informed by a multiplicity of factors – individual, group, organisational, inter-organisational, national, regional and global; they include:

* *ethics and value systems* (religion, culture, philosophy…),
* *internal environment* (management, staff, others impacted by decisions…),

- *groups* (teamwork, group dynamics, organisation development...),
- *technical systems* (technology, production systems...),
- *economics* (accounting, statistics, gross domestic product, inflation, demographics, global trends...),
- *external environment* (political, economic, social, technological, legal, environmental...),
- *trade* (tariffs/non-tariffs, financing, foreign exchange...),
- *individuals* (psychology, sociology, ethnicity, culture...).

Decision makers do not have the time to look at all these factors; however, as many as possible should be considered as objectively as possible for decisions with long-term implications.

Stages of Decision-Making

Simon (1977) identified three stages: intelligence, design and choice, followed by review.

1 *Intelligence* is identifying problems and defining those that require action. The question is 'what is the problem?' This involves problem identification, data collection, establishment of goals and evaluative criteria for the decision.
2 *Design* is formulating alternative courses of action; the question is 'what are the alternatives available?' based on consideration of various options.
3 *Choice* is the selection of an action by answering the question 'what is the best alternative?' Each alternative is examined in terms of costs and benefits

The *review* (monitoring and evaluation) complements the three stages by assessing the effectiveness of decision(s) and serves to assess past decisions and provide a basis for future ones.

The time devoted to each stage varies across situations – depending on simplicity/complexity, organisational level and from one manager to another, depending on their characteristics such as personality traits, experience and education.

Centralisation

Decisions vary from centralised to decentralised. Fayol, 1841–1925, (1930) believed that everything increasing the importance of subordinates' role is decentralisation, and everything reducing it is centralisation. The choice of centralisation or decentralisation is a question of degree, between making decisions at headquarters versus the division/subsidiary/branch level. Centralisation ensures consistency in decision-making but it may be difficult to get acceptance from lower levels and some decisions may be delayed. Decentralisation ensures acceptance and is responsive to immediate stakeholder demands but does not take the entire organisation into account. Usually, operational and tactical decisions are more decentralised while strategic decisions are more centralised.

Overall, centralisation/decentralisation depends on the history of the enterprise and the philosophy of management. Other factors include:

1 *Size* – it is more difficult to exercise control from the centre in large organisation.
2 *Degree of diversity* – it is easier to centralise decisions for similar activities than for diverse ones.
3 *Quality of superiors and subordinates* – if superiors are trusted and competent, centralisation will be accepted; if subordinates are competent and trusted, decentralisation will be preferred.

Decentralisation frees top management and to make strategic decisions, it encourages creativity and initiative at middle and lower levels and facilitates quick decision-making. It aids in the appraisal of performance, based on how the lower-level managers make decisions, and accomplish tasks. Some disadvantages are a lack of close coordination and control by top management, duplication of effort and activities in units, and difficulty in uniform application of policies and standards. Corporate services are often centralised while production decisions can be decentralised.

Improving Decision-Making

The essential aim in decision-making is to be objective and remove subjectivity/emotion. However, decision makers have biases including their academic/professional training, social background, religious beliefs, experience with similar situations, perceptual biases and any extraordinary circumstances. For example, in academia, the same case presented to academics from different disciplines leads to different interpretations and decisions. Marketing professors see marketing problems, HR professors HR problems and so on. Effective decision makers recognise their own biases and factor them into decisions. If we recognise and acknowledge bias, as a decision maker we can take a more objective and well-rounded view of the situation. The quality of decision-making can be improved in several ways:

- training and education to understand the process,
- adopting an open mind to avoid subjective biases,
- seeking relevant information including through research,
- networking with others in the organisation and outside,
- focusing on the mission, vision and values of the organisation to guide decisions.

Various aspects of decision and decision-making rely on communication. Effective communication is critical here as well as in many other aspects of organisations. We now look briefly at aspects of communication.

Communication

An important function of managers and leaders is to communicate the vision, mission, values and goals of the organisation, sharing both good and bad news, and communicating clearly, using the right media. Communication helps coordinate activities and empower members through sharing of insights and information that impact performance. Strategic plans should embed a communication strategy for success. Good communication enables everyone to act and contribute to the success of the organisation through individual and collective efforts.

Communication Model

Communication is a two-way process where sending and receiving responsibilities are shared by each party. According to Berlo (1960) a communication model comprises the source, message, channel/medium and receiver (abbreviated as SMCR) as shown in Table 5.1.

There are five personal factors (Communication Skills, Attitudes, Knowledge, Social System and Culture) pertinent to the sender (source) and the receiver. Structure, content, treatment and code comprise the 'message'. The channel comprises the human senses. A message is speech used or information conveyed, as well as the non-verbal messages exchanged through facial expressions, tone of voice, gestures and body language. For effective communication, the message should be well created and packaged, conveyed through a suitable

Table 5.1 Communication Model

Source	Message	Channel	Receiver
Communication skills	Elements	Seeing	Communication skills
Attitudes	Structure	Hearing	Attitudes
Knowledge	Content	Touching	Knowledge
Social system	Treatment	Smelling	Social system
Culture	Code	Tasting	Culture

medium (or media) so that it arrives to the receiver without distortion. Preferably, messages should be sent directly to the intended recipient(s) without passing through intermediaries to minimise distortion. The essence of communication is to ensure clarity and no communication breakdown. 'Perfect' communication occurs when the receiver ends up with the exact message the sender intended. Unfortunately, this is unlikely because of 'noise' throughout the communication system. Noise can be physical and occur because of technology that breaks down, a noisy environment, etc. It can also be psychological and occur because of the sender/receiver's attitudes, frame of mind and so on. Feedback provides a critical means to ensure that noise is identified, and minimised, and good communication takes place. Feedback is communication from the receiver back to the sender to indicate what message was received. Receivers should be willing to provide feedback, and senders should seek feedback to check and improve communication.

Communication occurs face-to-face, through electronic or print media, radio, television, the internet. Choice of medium is important because it should be affordable and accessible, for both the sender and receiver. In organisations, communication is often person to person through email or in-person, using memos or meetings. In this case, sensitive messages should be direct to the affected individual(s). The recipient of such a message finds this humane, respectful and considerate, and it is less likely to become distorted.

Distorted communication may occur when messages are sent through a third person. The third person may misunderstand the intention of the message or choose to 'spice it up' thus altering the meaning. In communal societies, like in Africa, information can be sent through multiple parties; however, confirmation is often sought from trusted individuals, usually elders, to ensure that correct information is transmitted. We next look at verbal and non-verbal communication.

Communication Methods

Communication can be verbal or non-verbal, spoken or written. For important communication, it is worth spending some time planning the communication method. Some messages are best spoken, some written and sometimes both are required. When we communicate in person, what we say verbally is important but the non-verbal cues can also carry many messages.

During verbal communication, intonation is important – neither too loud or too soft and appropriate for the nature of the communication. If someone is in danger, we may shout to get their attention while if we are giving private information we may whisper. We should generally 'speak with' rather than 'talk to' someone face-to-face or on the telephone, as this is seen as respectful and positive. People who feel you are 'talking to them' often 'shut down' and 'tune out', do not really listen and pay attention because their input does not seem important.

Non-verbal communication, often referred to as 'body language', communicates a great deal. For example, speaking while looking at the door indicates that you are not interested in the conversation and in a hurry to end it. Cultures are sometimes described as high or low context in terms of communication. Lower context cultures rely more on verbal communication while high context ones rely more on non-verbal. Generally, Western countries are relatively high context and Eastern countries are lower. African countries are described as relatively high; thus, we can expect non-verbal communication to play a relatively important role in communication in Africa. This is consistent with the communal culture where interpersonal relations are emphasised. Western managers will need to pay careful attention to non-verbal cues in the African context.

Effective Communication

We think communication is easy since we have always communicated, but it is complex, difficult and sometimes frustrating because of barriers we consciously or unconsciously put in the way of effective communication. There are several factors that contribute to in/effective communication:

Eye contact. During face-to-face communication, eye contact may be necessary, depending on the culture, or it may be avoided. In parts of Africa, it is described as 'wang teko' (luo language), 'imoni nyumu' (Tiriki language) meaning 'hard eye/dry eye' – a sign of disrespect.

In other cultures, lack of eye implies a lack of sincerity and that you are hiding something. Eye contact may depend on age; some cultures frown upon a younger person looking at an older person directly ('*mwana anyumira imoni*' meaning 'a child is showing me a dry eye' attracts punishment from a parent). This can negatively affect communications if one is unfamiliar with this culture and if lack of eye contact is interpreted as as hiding something or lying.

Listening is the key to communication. The receiver needs to pay attention to both verbal and non-verbal communication and ask for clarification if anything is unclear. We have all experienced our minds wondering and we lose track of what is being said, clearly communication cannot be effective then. Interrupting before the other party finishes is also a sign of poor listening, giving the impression that you are more interested in your ideas than what the other person is saying.

Silence is 'loud' and conveys a lot. Some cultures find silence upsetting because they are unsure what the other party is thinking. Other cultures spend substantial time silent, considering what has been said and how to respond. Americans are known for disliking silence and wanting to fill any silence, while the Japanese spend longer times silent. Silence is often associated with high context communication and should be interpreted in this light.

Information is important to communication and transfer of information is often the reason for communication at work. Too much information, or information overload, can, however, be a barrier to effective communication. There is only so much information that one can send or receive at one time, and the information should be relevant to decisions/activities. The Internet has resulted in an information explosion and the amount of information is generated and shared may obscure intended meaning. The sender should synthesise and communicate clear information to elicit the intended response. Concrete information is often easier to convey than abstract ideas.

Emotions are integral to communication. Positive emotions (happiness, love, joy) and negative emotions (sadness, anger) affect what and how we communicate, verbally and non-verbally. At work people may experience stress and various negative emotions that affect communication, as senders and receivers. To improve communication, we should be aware of our emotions when we communicate, and managers can encourage positive emotions as discussed in Chapter 4.

Filtering and perceptions influence what we send and what we receive. We select only what we want from a wide range of information and selection depends on our biases. We tend to avoid unpleasant information and sources. In organisations, an employee may avoid listening to a supervisor who has treated them harshly in the past and attribute negative motives to them. These cognitive biases need to be considered to ensure effective communication.

Disabilities affect communication. Physical issues such as stammering present impediments and are a challenge for the person with the impediment and those communicating with her/him. In such cases both parties need to be patient and speak and listen clearly and attentively. If the message is unclear, we can politely request repetition and give feedback to ensure we have understood the intended message.

Communication Direction

Consideration of what we are communicating and to whom is a major aspect of how we communicate. Communication to a superior will be different from that to a subordinate or co-worker. The information may be essentially the same, but we anticipate the effects of our communication and frame the communication with that in mind. The language and medium are based on these considerations. For example, sensitive information is usually communicated in-person and messages that require empathy or sympathy have special requirements.

We can think of the direction of communication as upward, downward and lateral. An upwards communication seeking assistance or information from a supervisor can take the form:

> *I will be most grateful to be advised on when I am likely to receive my*
> *performance appraisal feedback*
> Or *What is the feedback on my performance appraisal?*

Both say the writer is seeking information but the first is more appropriate for a supervisor. The second might seem rude and have a negative impact on the appraisal.

Sometimes we use subtler words to avoid seeming abrasive. A supervisor giving feedback (downward communication) could say

> *This output is not acceptable at your level*
> Or *I am confident you can do much better than this next time, let us*
> *discuss it more later*

The message is the same – dissatisfaction with performance. The first might cause a negative reaction in the receiver and might result in demotivation rather than improved performance. The second is more positive and incorporates the idea of working together to improve and is more likely to have a positive impact.

Upward and downward communications are generally more formal than communication. Lateral communication is among peers and may be relatively informal. We might say to a co-worker, *Give me a hand with this report* where we would request help more formally from our supervisor or subordinate.

Much communication in organisations takes place through what is often called the 'grapevine'. These communications are not formal or even intentional. They are the kind of communication that take place when you meet someone walking down the hall and say, "I heard that the boss wants to ...". Sometimes these communications are based on rumours and can be misleading, but the reality is that we all engage in them, and the grapevine can also serve as a positive way to disseminate information.

Formal appraisal meetings can provide particular communication challenges. When an employee's performance is below expectation, this must be communicated, but in such a way that it leads to better results in the future. Appraisal meetings should focus on understanding reasons for poor performance and ways to improve, through open discussion between subordinate and supervisor and a way of getting feedback from both the subordinate and supervisor.

Language/Culture in the African Context

There is limited information on language and cultural issues relevant to communication in Africa; nevertheless, some issues can be identified.

Language – Two people may technically speak the same language – the luhya, (Abaluhya) a Bantu community of western Kenya has 18 different dialects, including *Badiriji* (Tiriki), *Babukusu* (Bukusu) and *Banyore* that can make communication difficult. This is true in many parts of Africa. Many Africans also appear fluent in a European language, such as English or French, but these may not be the language they speak at home, and, in effect, the European language is a second language. This can make communication between Europeans and Africans more difficult, as the European communicates as though to another European. In some cases, the African counterpart may need a little more time to absorb the meaning and respond. In cases of different dialects, second languages, and other such situations, particular care in communication is required. Sometimes, communication needs to be repeated in different ways, using different words and more than one medium; say, a spoken message followed by a written one. In addition, feedback is especially important in these circumstances and both sender and receiver need to be particularly aware of non-verbal signals.

Cultural issues – Some beliefs and taboos in African societies affect communication. For example, open discussion about sex is generally taboo. Various roles in society are organised round gender in a stereotypic manner; for example, someone might say "cooking is not a matter for men" or is "a matter for women", a father might refer his daughter to the mother rather than have the daughter speak to him directly. Judy Mbugua says: In Africa, where I live, when a man visits a home and the husband/father is not in, the visitor goes away saying there was nobody at home – even though the wife (or wives) were there and were hospitable to him; and in one mosque in Nairobi, Kenya, a notice outside reads "Women and dogs are not allowed in the Mosque".

These cultural factors can be found in the workplace as well. In most of Africa, communication is often not very open, but this is changing. Internal grievances find expression through internal discussions (the 'grapevine') and the use of social media. From a legal standpoint, there may be whistleblower laws, suggestion boxes and other ways to express dissatisfaction. These may not be effective due to fear of victimisation.

Conclusion

Decision-making and communication are key aspects of organisational success. Decisions must be made all the time and at all levels, and good decisions lead to better outcomes while poor decisions can lead to failure. Understanding how decisions are made and the biases that affect them can result in better management. Communication also takes place all the time and at all levels, and good communication enhances management and increases performance. Understanding the components of communication and the different forms of communication as well barriers to effective communications improve our communication skills and help ensure we communicate what we want to communicate.

Review/Discussion

1 Discuss cultural barriers to communication in your community.
2 Explain how perceptual biases can be minimised in a typical decision situation.

3 Compare and contrast rational and behavioural decision-making.
4 Describe a situation where behavioural rather than rational decision-making is appropriate.
5 Explain the components of a model of communication.
6 Discuss 'spirituality is important in effective communication'.

Exercise: Choosing an IT Firm

Thanks to Dr. Theresa A. Chika-James & Brendon Black (MacEwan University).

Statistical reports have indicated Africa is behind the digital technological advancement of other emerging economies. Lack of coherent leadership and basic infrastructure, inadequate funds and lack of digital skills are some reasons for slow development. The lack of digital technology has impacted medical care, prolonged corruption and the ability of African economies to thrive globally. It has also led to the migration of the African skilled workers to other countries that offer better compensation and benefits.

Young Tesfay's is a case in point in the city of Asmara, Eritrea. Fresh out of Eritrea Institute of Technology with a degree in computer science, Tesfay started job hunting within Eritrea and other countries. While Tesfay is keen to find a challenging information technology (IT) job related to his field, he also wants commensurate pay to help his family in his hometown in Keren. Since, he is skilled in computer science, he has applied for jobs beyond Eritrea, Tesfay submits his resumes to the likes of Orange Asmara and Erimart in Eritrea; and three global technology companies – Amazon, Microsoft and IBM. Interestingly, within the first two weeks of submitting applications, Tesfay is invited to interviews by all five firms to take up a graduate entry position. The initial interviews were conducted virtually, and Tesfay came top amongst other job candidates. Tesfay was excited with the news of the job offers; however, he had to decide – should he start his IT career by signing an employment contract agreement with only one of the companies? This decision would be based on compensation and prospects for learning new technological innovations. After reviewing the offers from each company, Tesfay decided it would be best to work with the global firm Microsoft. The pay was good and assured he would receive employee benefits including health, dental and vision care, as well as other perks related to wellness programs. Professional development related to online, and in-person technical development courses were add-ons to his employment offer. There is little to no chance Tesfay will work in Eritrea.

Assignment

1 If you were Tesfay, would you take the job abroad? Why or why not?
2 How could Eritrea companies retain skilled talent, like Tesfay, from leaving the country?
3 What would you consider as essential technologies to get Tesfay to stay and work in Eritrea?
4 If you could solve any issue in Eritrea, and by extension, Africa, with a certain piece of technology, what would the issue be, and how can technology solve it?

References

Berlo, D. K. (1960). *The process of communication: An introduction to theory and practice.* New York, NY: Holt, Rinehart and Winston.
Cyert, R. M., & March, J. G. (1963). *A behavioral theory of the firm.* Prentice Hall/Pearson Education.
Fayol, H. (1930). *Industrial and general administration.* London: Sir I. Pitman & Sons, Ltd.
Hofstede, G. (2001). *Culture's consequences: Comparing values, behaviors, institutions, and organizations across nations*, 2nd ed. Thousand Oaks, CA: Sage. Retrieved April 2021 from https://digitalcommons.usu.edu/unf_research/53/
Okonedo, E. (2018). Decision-making practices in Africa. In U. Uzo & A. K. Meru (Eds.), *Indigenous management practices in Africa (advanced series in management* (Vol. 20, pp. 221–247). Bingley: Emerald Publishing Limited. DOI 10.1108/S1877-636120180000020012
Turpin, S. M., & Marais, M. A. (2004). "Decision-making: Theory and practice". *Orion, 20* (2), 143–160. DOI: 10.5784/20-2-12

6 Groups/Teams

Leaning Outcomes

After reading this chapter, you will be able to:

- Define and classify groups
- Describe In-groups/Out-groups
- Identify roles and norms in groups
- Explain group size, diversity and cohesiveness
- Describe group behaviour and development
- Discuss group effectiveness and social loafing
- Relate other factors to group decision-making
- Describe the characteristics of cross-functional, self-managed and virtual teams
- Explain how the African context influences groups/teams

Thought Starters

In order to realise continuity of learning during the COVID pandemic, one African Ministry of Health is providing expert guidelines – protocols to be followed to keep safe (social distancing, wearing masks and washing hands with running water) while the Ministry of Information and Communication technologies, through agencies under it, are collaborating with mobile and internet service providers to ensure affordable internet for teaching and learning. In this regard, the Kenya Education Network – an institution which supports internet connectivity for learning institutions – has negotiated subsidised internet connectivity packages to both faculty and students of learning institutions to enable them access to online teaching and learning as one of the collaborative responses to the COVID-19 pandemic.

DOI: 10.4324/9781003036838-6

Summary

This chapter defines and classifies groups, describes the concept of in-groups/out-groups and identifies group/team roles and norms. We examine the impact of group size, diversity and cohesiveness as well as the behaviour and development of groups. We also discuss the reality of working in groups/teams, both negative and positive. We consider group effectiveness and the impact of factors such as social loafing and group decision-making, as well as cross-functional, self-managed and virtual teams. We also discuss cultural issues in teams and relate group/team functioning to the African context.

Defining Groups and Teams

A group is several people/objects located/assembled/classed together. A team is a group of people collaborating on a task to achieve an objective. Teamwork is important in organisations of all types. The collaborative effort of team members means tasks are carried out more efficiently than if performed by individuals; particularly, complex tasks require team effort where members contribute diverse expertise, skills and insights. A group collaborating on a task are also subject to group dynamics, such as conflict, negatively affecting performance. African countries have been described as 'relatively collective', 'collaborative' and 'community-oriented'; thus, understanding the way groups/teams work may be especially pertinent in the African context.

One aspect of groups that is prevalent everywhere relates to group make-up and how this leads to in-group versus out-group attitudes.

In-Group/Out-Group

People define themselves relative to the group(s) to which they belong. An in-group is one where you feel included and comprises people who identify with each other based on education, gender, geography, race, religion, etc., or because of shared attitudes and values. The in-group/out-group psychological disposition of individuals in a social setting makes them identify with certain groups where they belong and feel comfortable, and others where they do not, as shown in Figure 6.1.

An individual perceives who s/he is and decides which social group(s) they want to belong to. They join the preferred group (in-group), if accepted by the group, and categorise others as not part of their group (outgroup). They see the world as a dichotomy, 'us/we' versus 'them/they', making intergroup comparisons which guide behaviour. This can

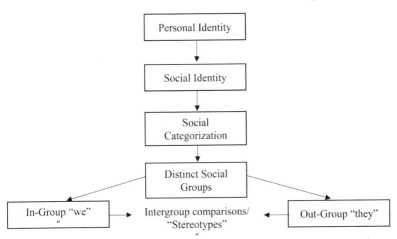

Figure 6.1 Social Identity Process.

affect team performance. If a team member perceives a co-worker as 'out-group' or team members do not see themselves as 'in-group', the team will not be cohesive, leading to the ineffectiveness. Selection of team members, where appropriate, can consider psychological and sociological dispositions of team members to the cohesiveness of an in-group to foster collaborative teamwork, and training can be used to encourage this. In African countries, if ethnic differences are a factor, this can have negative consequences and affect team efforts and training programmes may be needed to overcome in-group/out-group biases.

Studies suggest that individuals empathise when an in-group member is harmed, but not when a member of an out-group is the one harmed. Supporters of Manchester United (UK), Ashante Kotoko (Ghana) and Green Eagles (Nigeria) see themselves as the in-group members while supporters of the rivals are the out-group members. If a team member is hurt the in-group will sympathise and the out-group may actually applaud. This draws on social identity theory (Tajfel & Turner, 1979) proposing that groups (social class, family, football team, etc.) are an important source of pride and self-esteem; giving a sense of social identity/belonging to the social world. Members of an in-group will seek to find negative aspects of an out-group, enhancing their self-image. The implication is that categorising others in terms of race, gender, social status, etc., relies on stereotypes and leads to discrimination. Some literature describes African countries as practicing 'tribalism' where allegiance to one's 'tribe' is especially important.

This suggests that the formation of 'tribal in-groups' is likely in such cases and may lead to discrimination in hiring, mentoring, promoting and other organisational reward systems.

Today diversity is described in a positive manner and we seek common ground to collaborate irrespective of diversity. Ideas of cultural sensitivity and diversity competency are valued in a global business environment. Teams can be globally dispersed; hence, the need to work with people from different cultural and professional background. Even in smaller organisations, diversity encourages a range of ideas and helps engage with diverse stakeholders, including customers, suppliers and lenders. The in-group/out-group mentality described previously can make it difficult to embrace diversity and organisational leaders may have to make special efforts in this regard to reap the benefits that diversity provides.

We have not identified African studies dealing with these issues; however, anecdotally, in Africa, decisions on employment and political appointments are made based on in-group considerations including ethnicity/tribe, kinship/family, religion and so on, rather than on merit. This is counterproductive because such appointments are not based on competence and affect work outcomes, and are perceived to be discriminatory, demotivating other employees who merit such appointments. Managers in Africa need to be aware of and manage these dynamics. In small and family-owned organisations, preferring in-group or family members for certain positions is often based on trust and this may have some practical importance, but the potential negative consequences also need to be recognised.

Group Characteristics

Establishing group norms and roles is crucial for the proper functioning of groups. These should be clarified before commencing an activity because they will guide the activity towards the group's objectives. Failure to do this can lead to undesirable group dynamics including social loafing, time wasting, diversionary activities, at the expense of the group's objectives.

Norms – expectations of group members, such as codes of conduct, provide 'ground rules' that guide member's conduct. Every group develops its customs, rituals, habits and expectations and these influence how members communicate, including expected courtesies and decorum. Norms support or hinder achievement of a group's goals (at a retreat, staff members switch off mobiles, go to breakfast together at 7 am, and do not interrupt others, facilitating the progress of the retreat).

Roles – specific responsibilities and accountabilities for group members (at the staff retreat, one member is assigned as timekeeper to alert the group when an activity is to start and end). When designing teams, size, diversity and cohesiveness are important considerations.

Size – optimal size is not too large or small. If the group is large, loafing is more likely and co-ordination is difficult, if very small, diversity is curtailed, decisions do not benefit from varied viewpoints, and members may be overburdened. Finding the optimal size depends on the objectives of the group.

Diversity – variations in gender, expertise, culture and so on brings more insights to the group and enhances performance. Homogeneous groups are prone to groupthink, because all members share a similar perspective and way of thinking, resulting in poor decisions. Diverse viewpoints provide comparisons of different approaches and solutions to problems.

Cohesiveness – means sticking together that is based on a shared vision, goals/objectives, understanding responsibilities and accountabilities, a positive attitude to the team assignment and mutual support/respect for each other.

The composition of the team is important and the leader and members should be selected carefully. Composition takes into account the required skills and expertise to achieve objectives, and the leader's characteristics. Skills/expertise need to be available for all activities. The leader needs interpersonal skills (to guide members and resolve conflicts), conceptual skills (to understand the big picture) and analytical skills (for specific activities).

The characteristics of the group/team lead to interactions among members, broadly called group dynamics.

Group Dynamics

Group dynamics relates to psychological and social factors when people interact in a group setting, and are the attitudinal and behavioural characteristics of a group. These include group formation, structure and process, and functioning, and, various personality, role, motivation and expectation related issues.

Groups are often described as going through the following stages:

Forming: This is the beginning when members are new to a work assignment (organisation) or activity (informal group). During this stage members get to know each other, formally and informally.

Storming: Members look for other similar individuals and form sub-groups. This creates differences and tensions and there is conflict regarding roles and levels of power in the group.

Norming: Members become more concerned with task performance and sub-groups open up and become more inclusive. Establishing norms solidifies group identity and cohesion and establishes leadership patterns.

Performing: Groups that successfully go through the process become fully functional and see themselves as a group and get involved in the task. Each member makes contributions and the leader is an integral part of the group. Group norms are followed and pressure is exerted to ensure group longer-term viability and effectiveness.

This is often presented as a sequence, but in reality groups may go through several stages at the same time, and a performing group may experience sub-groups and conflicts, and norming may be continuous. Group dynamics must be managed effectively so that they do not to negatively affect its functioning and impair the realisation of its objectives. Conflict is a particular issue to be managed or avoided.

Structuring the team in terms of member roles, team leadership, modes of working and communication, and planning operations reduces strife and minimises possibilities of conflict. When conflicts occur the team leaders and members need to identity causes – role ambiguity, role conflict, personality clashes, etc., discuss them openly, and resolve them mutually by honestly confronting the causes and agreeing on actions to avoid future conflicts. For example, a team member with a high need for achievement (personality, motivation) can be assigned a more challenging role. Conflict can be partially minimised by clarifying the vision and mission of the team, and objectives, actions and responsibilities of each member.

Types of Groups/Teams

There are various types of teams. Some of the most common are:

Work teams – including employee teams and task force. Employee teams can be a group in a department that collaborate on tasks aligned with achieving a departmental objective; say developing a new promotion mix for a product within the marketing department. A taskforce is set up to execute a particular task, with a start and end time, working within specified terms of reference;

for example, investigating a disaster or carrying out a fact-finding mission to make recommendations to guide decisions.

Management teams – refers to a group charged with the responsibility of guiding an organisation to achieve its objectives on a day-to-day and long-term basis. This can be senior managers and directors, with the chief executive officer usually the secretary of the board or it can be a group of middle-level managers/operational managers who, respectively, run units and carry out day-to-day operations, ensuring that activities are aligned with the organisation's objectives.

Project teams – are set up to complete a specific project, with a defined beginning and end. A consultancy is a project, worked on by a team to deliver client expectations, on contractual terms. The team is constituted according to the scope and terms of reference of the consultancy, with members having expertise in specified areas, and each team member responsible/accountable for specific activities and outputs. Accountability for results must be ensured by every member because reporting to the client is specified in the schedule of deliverables. Further, delays have financial and other undesirable implications. Communication is critical – among team members, between the team leader and the project manager (if different), and between project manager and client.

In addition, groups/teams differ in makeup and how they interact.

Cross-Functionality

Cross-functional teams collaborate on an assignment requiring expertise from various functional areas, requiring diverse expertise and skills. Communication across functions/disciplines is important. Experts, say engineers, doctors, lawyers have domain specific language/terminology which can prove a barrier to others, say, in marketing who may not understand the terminology. To ensure no communication breakdown team members need to communicate in a language understood by all.

Many current problems, such as COVID-19, require interventions from a multidisciplinary perspective with medics, information/communication technology, psychologists, legal experts, etc., need to collaborate in addressing a complex problem. COVID-19 response teams in universities include faculty members, human resource personnel, student leaders, administrative staff, religious leaders and doctors to address the problem using their various expertise and charting a way forward. At the country level, ministries of health, education and information/communication technologies collaborate to combat the pandemic ensuring teaching and learning progress using technology online approaches.

Self-Management

A self-managed team is a group of employees collectively responsible for the projects they work on, and specific employees – who are not necessarily managers – take leadership over tasks and initiatives based on their expertise, rather than hierarchy/title. Teams are responsible and accountable for all/most aspects of producing a product or delivering a service. A self-managed team carries out tasks, such as planning and scheduling the workflow, and managing annual leave and absence, in addition to technical tasks. Many companies use such teams because they motivate employees to take ownership and, allowing people to make decisions, means they reach new levels of engagement and participation. These teams may be particularly appropriate for smaller businesses because this frees top managers/owners for more strategic activities.

Use of self-managed teams relies on a culture of trust, where those at the top believe employees will do their best for the organisation. These teams require employees who are able and comfortable taking responsibility and accepting accountability. This may not be the norm in many African firms, given the colonial past, relatively high power distance (decisions made at the top) and preference for risk avoidance (avoid responsibility/accountability). To benefit from the advantages of such teams, some African organisations may want to implement training/development programmes aimed at changing attitudes.

A challenge in self-managed teams is social loafing – a reduction in effort because there is a sense one will not be held accountable for results. The causes of loafing include:

- lack of motivation when the team members are not adequately rewarded or do not think the group activity is worthwhile,
- diffusion of responsibility so a member feels less personally accountable for a task, and believes individual efforts have little impact on outcomes,
- large group size where it is difficult to identify if a member is not engaged on the task.

Failing to take responsibility because "I will not be caught" needs to be addressed directly and social loafers need to be held to account. This can be difficult in self-managed teams, because the leaders may not have position power in the normal sense (i.e., title), or coercive or reward power (ability to sanction or reward). In small and family firms there is the added challenge that team members are likely on close personal terms. The issue should therefore be discussed in advance with team members, agreeing on a process for identifying and addressing loafing behaviours.

Virtual Teams

Virtual teams are teams that are not physically together and work remotely. The COVID-19 pandemic has dramatically increased the number of people working virtually, around the world, and the number of people working in virtual teams. The general belief is that this will continue post-pandemic and understanding how these teams operate will become more important. We expect there will be substantial research on these teams' effectiveness in the coming years. Currently, anecdotally, some people are very positive about virtual work and virtual teams, others are negative or in-between. It seems likely that personal attributes, such as attitudes, personality, values impact on reactions to remote work and that cultural characteristics will influence the factors that make these teams effective.

In the past, virtual teams were often formed for a temporary period to implement a particular task, solve a specific problem or work on new product development, where the skills/experience/expertise needed were not in the same place. This dynamic implied little prior history, and roles and responsibilities of team members changed with each virtual team. A person was a leader in one team and a minor, supportive member in another. Typically, virtual team structures were non-hierarchical and decentralised, with members focusing on lateral and informal information exchanges to accomplish objectives. Virtual teams may become more permanent in the future but other dynamics will likely remain.

Virtual teams come in many different forms. For example, they may be geographically dispersed but homogeneous in other ways such as the LEAD project team, all academics, with researchers from Ghana, Egypt, Nigeria, Uganda, Kenya, US, West Indies and Canada, or they may be in one location representing different companies and countries. Local virtual teams are usually people from the same company working virtually (such as remote working in our universities brought about by the COVID-19 pandemic) while global virtual teams are usually located in different countries.

Different types of teams require different structures and processes, but generally to be successful:

- Virtual teams need a leader. The leader may not be one in the hierarchical sense, but someone needs to take on the role of guiding the team, articulating a vision, confirming objectives and so on.
- Milestones are important and tangible evidence of success should be shared with all members.
- Some member(s) with good organisational skills need to keep track of team progress and outcomes and a 'keeper of information' needs to be an explicit task.
- Communications, particularly where there are language differences, is a challenge. The language used has to be understood by all members, but it may not be everyone's first language, and team members have to be sensitive to the difficulties others may face in communicating verbally.
- Non-verbal communication is complex because current technology does not allow easy identification of facial expressions, body language and the like. This is exacerbated by cultural differences, for example, where some members tend to remain silent and others tend to contribute actively to discussions.
- It is critical to identify ways to encourage social interactions among members of a virtual team.

Overall, we recommend that virtual teams watch carefully for evidence of problems and agree that these should be identified and discussed openly by the whole group. Some team members may be uncomfortable with this, and it is part of the leader's role to encourage such discussions. For example, in African countries where younger members naturally defer to older ones, if may not be easy for a young person to say something like "I feel no-one is listening to my ideas". The leader should communicate regularly with all members with a view to uncovering any issues like this. Virtual remote work may be particularly challenging in the African context because of the importance of collective and communal values. It can be difficult to develop feelings of community when people are not physically together. Virtual work can also foster the in-group/out-group dynamic, with those in the in-group interacting more and sharing information in such a way that those in the out-group are isolated. Many people believe that the pandemic started a major move to virtual remote work, but that it will not end with the end of the pandemic. African managers will need to pay close attention to designing, managing and leading groups and teams working remotely, to avoid the potential negative results and benefit from the positive ones.

Succeeding in Groups/Teams

To work effectively in teams, clarity of the vision/objective of the team should be shared with team members. This ensures that members remain focused, and the leader has a responsibility of refocusing the attention and objectives in case of need. Communication should be regular and open to ensure all members are reading from the same script. Further, a team member should seek clarifications if something is not clear and support fellow team members when necessary, while focusing on her/his assigned role and accountability. Courtesy is crucial in team success – punctuality and submitting competed assignments on time, apologising for delays or lateness for meetings, providing information regarding absence or lateness in advance and so on.

When tasks are complex, stress can set in and management of stress in teams becomes necessary. Clear understanding of acceptable/good results is paramount but takes some time to crystallise. Team members should spend time reflecting on desired outcomes, tasks to be performed, skills/expertise required and responsibility and accountability for the assignment in the context of its scope. The aim is common understanding of expectations, how those will be met and who will be in charge of what aspects of the assignment. Teams are set up to collaborate to achieve objectives working on a task; therefore, ensuring clarity from the onset, assigning responsibilities and accountabilities to each team leader/member, clarifying expectations and seeking team member views so details are clear and accepted is paramount. Reporting mechanisms and frequency are also needed. We present next describe team roles and communication in teams as important aspects of teams.

Team Roles

Various roles are present in teams. Ensuring appropriate assignment of roles leads to success of teams. Five of such team roles are as follows:

> *Leader role* – provides direction, vision and motivation to the team, and also creates rules that guide the working of the team in consultation with team members. In addition, the leader assigns various roles depending on the expertise, skills and attitudes of team members and ensures that team values are maintained.

Creative director role – provides energy by thinking out of the box and introduces unique initiatives in the team that promote development and enhancement of team effort.

Facilitator role – is without formal authority but helps the team in making effective decisions.

Coach role – has the role of providing one-on-one support to a team member after the team member has been trained. The leader can also perform the role of a coach.

Member role – participates in meetings and perform tasks that are assigned to them. A team member participates in brainstorming and generation of ideas among other support to the team.

Communication in Teams

Part of the planning for execution of a team effort is communication within the team. Effective communication mechanism should be developed and implemented. Communication· methods can include communicating through updates and reports; memos and through face-to-face means and also through project or management review meetings; or even site meetings.

Effective teams have clear goals, effective leadership, good communication, assigned roles/responsibilities/accountability and clear reporting mechanisms. Such team are cohesive and maintain harmonious working relations and have positive attitudes toward teamwork. A transparent reward system is also motivational and leads to effectiveness. Finally, the team leader should treat all members fairly and equitably to avoid conflict and resentments.

Pitfalls in Groups/Teams

Teams are not without pitfalls. Some of the pitfalls arise from team composition where the skill set and expertise is mismatched with the task at hand, incompetent team leadership where the leader may be inadequate in either conceptual, analytical, negotiation and/or interpersonal skills including communication skills. Some pitfalls include:

High need for achievement – If some team members have a high need for achievement, they may be impatient or demotivated when results are not forthcoming as fast as they would like, and they may be impatient with co-workers. Team leaders should identify such members and assign them additional responsibilities, such as putting together reports from other team members, so that they will not feel idle.

Slower members – All team members on an assignment may not be able to work at the same pace. If one or two team members are slower than others, this will hold back progress. The team leader should talk directly with the concerned member to discuss areas of weakness and how the team can help them meet the team's expectations. Language issues can cause some members to seem slower than others, because they have difficulty following discussions and effective communication can help overcome these difficulties.

Leadership – The team leader needs to have both technical and social skills. If a leader does not understand the requirements of the task s/he cannot be effective and if s/he does not engender social cohesion the team will not function as a team. It is important that the leader also recognises shortcomings in team members and takes corrective measures to ensure effective participation of all members (in exceptional cases, releasing a team member for non-performance). Attributes of *Ubuntu* may be particularly relevant to ensuring a well-functioning team in the African context.

Groupthink – This is a phenomenon where team members make decisions based on a desire for cohesiveness – i.e., everyone goes along with a decision even when they do not agree in order to minimise conflict. This can result in ineffective decision-making. Encouraging dissenting voices helps minimise groupthink, and identifying domineering team members ensures they do not intimidate others and override their contributions. Groupthink may be particularly relevant in the African context because of the collective and collaborative cultural values, and the respect for age and wisdom may lead to some members playing a dominant role and others simply going along with their decisions.

Much work in organisations is carried out in groups. In fact it is unusual for someone to work individually, without at least some reliance on others for input. Teams are groups of employees, but we usually think of a team as working closely together on a shared task or towards a common goal. Groups and teams have become even more common in today's organisations; therefore, it is important for managers to consider potential challenges and ensure they are resolved.

Conclusion

We described various types of teams including management and work team, cross-functional teams, and also virtual teams, which have become very important in the face of global pandemic – COVID-19. All these types of teams have various factors in common: an objective to meet, an imperative to collaborate, need for effective leadership and communication, and group dynamics some of which may be negative such as conflict. Conflict is inevitable when a group of people are working together in a collaborative manner to achieve an objective; however, conflicts should be resolved as a way of managing stress which is associated with complex projects requiring cross-functional teams and which place big demands on team members. Stress should be effectively managed in order to ensure success of teamwork.

Review/Discussion

1 Discuss the advantages and disadvantages of in-group/out-group classifications.
2 Explain how you can effectively manage virtual team.
3 Discuss the statement 'conflict is inevitable in teams/groups'.
4 Explain and critique the Berlo communication model.
5 Based on your personal experience, describe how decisions are made in your African context, and how this relates to the concepts in this chapter.

Exercise: Mini Case

Time is running out to submit a consultancy assignment report. Deadlines had been agreed upon and each member committed to turn in their sections of the report. The due date is fast approaching. A review meeting is called to take stock of the progress.

The team leader begins "Good morning team. I hope we are all fine. As you will recall, we agreed to turn in inputs last week including during a retreat on this assignment; however, we are falling behind time. Let us hear comments from the team".

A team member replied "It is too early in the morning, for you as the team leader to speak that firmly. In fact, I am not motivated".

"This is about work! Deadlines were agreed in our review meeting and we need to deliver to the client. We need to proactively seek information that we need to complete our respective tasks between the meetings rather than waiting to raise them during reviews like this one", the leader responded firmly.

Another team member said "I suggest we work as a team and if a member needs assistance, they can ask any member for assistance. This will fast-track the work". After this meeting the team leader received an earlier late submission from the non-performing team member. The submission fell short of expectations. He replied to the 'demotivated' team member: "… this submission is late, I suggest that we be adhering to agreed timelines; please check the format by John (not real name), adapt your input, finalise and submit". The member replied that "If you are not satisfied with my performance, tell me whom to hand over to". Might it have been *Khutsugani ikhumba ni shisudi* – we are gathered as *ikhumba* and *shisudi* meaning we are not homogeneous, loosely translated to mean "we are not in one accord – reading from different scripts"?

Assignment

1 Discuss the team dynamics implied by this situation.
2 Explain how the performance of the team can be improved.
3 Describe what you would do in this situation if you were team leader.

References

Tajfel, H., & Turner, J. C. (1979). An integrative theory of inter-group conflict. In W. G. Austin & S. Worchel (Eds.), *The social psychology of inter-group relations* (pp. 33–47). Monterey, CA: Brooks/Cole.

Online Sources

"Establishing group norms". Retrieved from https://www.berea.edu/brushy-fork-institute/establishing-group-norms/
"What is social identity". Retrieved from https://zaqinixiwyge.instituteforzen-therapy.com/what-is-social-identity-25059bd.html

7 Leadership and Influence

Learning Outcomes

After completing this chapter, you will be able to:

- Explain the difference between managers and leaders
- Describe and illustrate various leadership theories
- Define and explain mentoring and empowerment
- Explain the importance of trust, justice, ethics in leadership
- Describe the bases and uses of power
- Delineate the relationship between power, politics and influence
- Present Africa-specific cultural issues pertinent to leadership, referring to LEAD

Thought Starters

Leaders are important today because "the success or failure of all organizations rests on the perceived quality of the people at the top" (p. 2), and "to those in high places, lying or cheating was tantamount to professional suicide" (p. 3); furthermore, "shame and embarrassment have yielded to arrogance and bald-faced denials, no matter how damning the evidence", and "greed, timidity, and lack of vision are rampant among the current crop of pseudoleaders; we need leaders who will rise above those tawdry standards" (Bennis, 1989, pp. 2–3).
Fish rots from the head ...

Summary

In this chapter, we distinguish between managers and leaders, present leadership theories, evolving from more traditional to current thinking. We describe mentoring and empowerment and explain the role of trust, justice and ethics as part of leadership. We also discuss the

DOI: 10.4324/9781003036838-7

bases of power and how to use power to influence followers, differentiating among power, politics and influence. We conclude with Africa-specific issues pertinent to leadership with reference to the Leadership Effectiveness in Africa and the Diaspora (LEAD) project.

Introduction

Many people lament the absence of effective leaders, reflected in the mistrust of those in positions of authority, and the search for leadership effectiveness continues (Senaji et al., 2020). Marques (2020, p. 3) says the practice of inclusive leadership is not a luxury, not even an option today. It is required for any leader wanting to take her/his organisation to greater heights. A globalised world and discerning customers mean leaders must learn quickly and harness the efforts of all organisation members like an orchestra conductor, ensuring an inclusive harmonious whole of all players.

People ask, 'who are great leaders?' They are found across the society, and have a vision and unwavering conviction. Examples often cited are Martin Luther King Jr. and Nelson Mandela. Leadership is often lonely, and leaders reflect on how to move their followers to the next level of achievement. In Africa, positive examples are *Osagyefo* Kwame Nkrumah, the Pan-Africanist who envisioned African unity that led to the Organization of African Unity (now African Union) and *Mwalimu* Julius Nyerere who advocated for an African continental government as necessary and inevitable (note that others saw this as 'a nightmare'). Society has also had leaders who are viewed negatively. Perhaps another word is needed for people in leadership positions who use their position for negative outcomes?

Some Examples of Negative Leadership at the National Level in Africa

Africa has had negative leaders, including dictators such as Idi Amin in Uganda, Jean-Bedel Bokassa in the Central Africa Republic and several 'life presidents' who believe that they are 'God's gift to man'. There have been leaders who changed constitutions so they could 'die on the throne'. In many cases, they end badly. A former strongman of Zaire found a 'resting place' somewhere in Rabat, Morocco yet he was known as "the cock that crowed and left no hen untouched" back home. Idi Amin, 'the conqueror of the British Empire', died in exile in Saudi Arabia. This failure in leadership is not only a preserve of Africa; there are examples elsewhere, such as Adolf Hitler in Nazi Germany.

Transformational and charismatic leadership are usually considered effective; however, these are not necessarily good, in a moral sense. Mahatma Gandhi and Adolf Hitler are both considered charismatic leaders, yet they represent opposing worldviews and societal values, with Gandhi almost universally revered and Hitler reviled. Negative leadership is found in organisations as well, and it must be dealt with through effective oversight by boards of directors.

Manager Versus Leader

Management and leadership occur in all types of organisations. They share attributes but are conceptually distinct.

Managers seek to optimise scarce resources (people, money, equipment/machines, etc.) to achieve organisational objectives – management is achieving desired results within resource and time constraints. Leaders are influencers; motivating and inspiring followers to work towards a vision (not necessarily within formal organisation settings). Managers are responsible for a unit (department, function, organisation, etc.); they plan, ensure an appropriate structure is in place, see resources are available to achieve plans, monitor performance and take corrective action to reach desired goals. Leadership is more, as it incorporates developing a shared vision throughout a group and stimulating others to behave in desired ways. While these differences are important, the terms are often used interchangeably. We focus on leadership; however, we often refer to leadership in the context of management and as an activity that managers perform, along with others. Managers/leaders are responsible for ensuring that people in their unit work in ways to achieve planned strategies and goals.

Effective leaders/managers adopt styles that enhance this achievement. Broadly defined, leadership is the ability to get others to behave as the leader wishes. There are many processes and structures that enhance organisational functioning, but finally, organisations succeed or fail because of leadership, and they cannot function well without effective leaders.

Leadership embodies a long-term vision, whereas management has a short-term orientation focused on operating within annual budgets and allocating resources – human, time, money, physical – within that context. Particularly in changing environments, characterised by instability, turbulence and unpredictability, executives, managers and operational staff need to anticipate changes and adjust/adapt, making both management and leadership essential to organisational success.

Leadership Theories

Leadership theories seek to explain what makes an effective leader. Theory has developed from the Great Man approach, through consideration of traits and behaviours, to situational/contingency theories which incorporate contextual issues and transformational ideas. Related are leader behaviours including authoritarian and participative behaviours, leader-member exchanges, transactional and transformational approaches and charisma. Most of these were developed in the West but have application in the African context. The earlier theories (Great Man and traits) appear to have informed the choice of leaders in Africa during precolonial and colonial periods, but this is slowly changing. In parts of Africa, state leadership positions are inherited (e.g., Eswatini and Lesotho kingdoms); in others, families or clans dominate these positions. Other factors, wealth, the ability to foresee future events, education compared to others are also associated with leadership positions. Wealth remains an important predictor of state power and leadership in many African countries.

Great Man/Traits theories were prominent in the early 1900s. Carlyle collected biographies of great men through history to illustrate the 'great man' concept, while Stogdill focused on identifying effective leadership traits/characteristics. The assumption is that great leaders are born with traits that enable them to rise and lead; and they come to the fore when there is a need for them. Leadership traits included intelligence, charisma, courage, risk taking, physical characteristics and so on. Over time it was found that people with these traits/characteristics did not necessarily succeed as leaders and some effective leaders did not have them, and this theory fell out of favour. Nevertheless, there are people who continue to say things like s/he 'looks like a leader'. When Nelson Mandela walked out of prison in South Africa many onlookers made this remark about him. The idea that leaders are made not born emerged in the mid-1900s with a focus on how leaders behave.

Behavioural theories initially proposed two sets of behaviours – task (*initiating structure*) and employee/people (*consideration*). An effective leader would focus on either task characteristics or attending to employee welfare. These studies initially did not consider situational factors and assumed a particular behaviour accounted for effectiveness. Empirically, this was not always the case and this limitation led to contingency/situational theories.

Contingency theories. Early work posited that effective leadership behaviour should be adapted to the situation, including the characteristics of the leader, the follower/employee and the task. In Fiedler's (1964) model, a situation is described as 'favourable' when followers have necessary skills, the task is structured and the leader can reward performance and has support from superiors and peers. If employees' skills are limited, tasks complex, and there is little support for the leader the situation is 'unfavourable'. An employee-oriented leadership is best for complex tasks and unskilled employees, a task approach works best for structured tasks and experienced employees. This work evolved into the understanding that no one leadership style was best and that leaders could adopt both task and people orientations together and could change depending on the situation.

Recent theories cover a variety of additional ideas.

Transformational/charismatic leadership is concerned with inspiration, visioning, intellectually stimulating followers and focusing on followers' welfare. Transformational leadership empowers and unlocks followers' potential to achieve the best they can, given their talents and skills. This leadership is developmental and intended to involve followers and motivate them to achieve. It is concerned with followers' welfare and inner being, including emotions, where an emotional bond is created between the leader and the followers. African examples are Nelson Mandela, Kwame Nkurumah, Julius Nyerere and Raila Amolo Odinga – these leaders have followers who support them through adversities and difficult circumstances.

LMX (Leader-Member Exchange) posits that the quality of the relationship between the leader and each follower is different; some relationships are of 'higher quality' than others. These relationships are called vertical dyads. Consider three followers A, B, C and a leader (L), the relationships A-L, B-L, C-L depend on exchanges that occur, the trust between L and each follower, and the nature of feedback that followers receive from L and vice versa. 'Quality' also depends on the unique abilities of each follower which can enhance the performance of the leader. The more a follower has initiative and provides support – ideas and suggestions – to the leader, the higher the relationship quality of the dyad. Leaders can evaluate dyads to ensure they are productive.

Role theory proposes that behaviour is guided by expectations. It concerns how leaders/followers define their own roles and actions/activities in an organisation, and how they perceive the roles of others in achieving organisational goals. A leader may see her/his role as articulating a vision, inspiring/motivating followers while followers see their role as implementing actions specified in a plan. If the leader and followers have clarity regarding their roles, they mutually reinforce each other in pursuit of organisational goals. If roles are clearly defined and understood role conflict and resource wastage are reduced, leading to better performance. Role conflict occurs if there are varying expectations of leaders or if a leader is perceived as not playing the appropriate/expected role. Role clarity means legitimate expectations regarding members' outputs, forming the basis of performance management.

Path-Goal Theory focuses on a leader showing followers how to achieve goals, providing resources, and ensuring that rewards are linked to achieving goals, based on followers' expectations. House and Dessler (1974) argued that if a leader clarifies goals and makes them attractive, followers will be satisfied, motivated and perform well and the leader will be accepted. Four leader behaviours were identified:

Directive – the leader tells followers what to do (this is appropriate when the follower have low levels of skills and where tasks are complex).

Supportive – the leader assists followers with task execution by considering their needs and clarifying what needs to be done.

Participative – followers are invited to give suggestions on the best way to carry out tasks.

Achievement oriented – followers are considered experts and self-motivated and the leader simply identifies challenging goals and provides access to resources, and lets employees complete their tasks independently.

The Globe Study is one of the most comprehensive studies of leadership around the world (Global Leadership and Organizational Behavior Effectiveness – House et al., 2004) and began with research in 62 countries. This research found that charismatic/value-based leadership, including visionary, inspirational and team-building dimensions was universally endorsed. In contrast, leaders described as self-protective, ensuring the leader's security, self-centred and encouraging in-group/out-group distinctions was universally seen as ineffective. These results held in African countries included in the study. The skill of oration was included as important in African countries, and modesty and humane orientations received high scores. An individualistic and autonomous leadership style was seen as less positive.

The study of leadership has been conducted from a variety of perspectives. Each provides insights into effective leadership. There are a number not discussed here for space reasons, and the reader is encouraged to examine these further.

For example, inclusive leadership (Senaji et al., 2020) arises from the diversity and inclusivity imperatives that we find in organisations today. Leaders in Africa should be equipped with the necessary skills and attitudes for the global business environment where cultural sensitivity and the attendant appreciation of diversity and inclusivity are paramount.

Leadership in developing countries has been described as a reciprocal relationship between the leader and her/his subordinates based on relatively high power distance (as well as high uncertainty avoidance and collectivism). Leaders are expected to take responsibility for the welfare of their subordinates, and, in turn, subordinates are loyal to their leaders and perform the tasks they are assigned. Leadership in this context is essentially autocratic and subordinates may believe that leaders know what needs to be done and look up to leaders simply because they are leaders. This style is often found in African organisations.

There are several aspects of leadership which also contribute to effectiveness, we discuss two of these next.

Mentoring

Mentoring is about creating successors. Leaders are responsible for mentoring others to be leaders, and organisations rely on this to develop future leaders/managers. Effective mentoring means the leader can concentrate on 'higher ideals' including articulating a vision, identifying opportunities to improve well-being and organisational excellence. Leaders/managers who do not mentor cannot be promoted because they have not prepared anyone to take over.

In various religious traditions, there is reference to mentoring. In Christianity, Moses mentored Joshua and Jesus mentored Peter to succeed him. In Islam, mentoring is called *al-halaqah* (group gathering) and *usrah* (family system) where *naqib* (leader) or *murabbi* (educator) is responsible for delivering information, discussing and sharing knowledge with his/her member (mentee). In Buddhism the mentor–disciple relationship is "to enable people to develop to their fullest potential" (https://tricycle.org/magazine/mentorship-in-sgi-buddhism/). In Judaism, *chavruta* translates to partnership, or fellowship. *Chaver* means friend and refers to a two-sided relationship based on learning, sought-after between a leader and mentees. Traditional African culture encourages mentorship; for example, the Tiriki of western Kenya, identify *mudiri* as the mentor of boys during their rite of passage to 'becoming men' – responsible for their education and induction as men when they rejoin society.

One important characteristic of a mentor is generosity, through sharing insights, time, knowledge and experiences. A mentor creates time to interact with followers, provide guidance and listen to concerns/ needs. A 'too busy leader', without time for followers, cannot mentor. A mentor offers praise when deserved, and constructively corrects when necessary. A positive attitude, high moral standing, integrity and professionalism are hallmarks of a mentor. Effective mentoring also depends on followers' willingness to be mentored; some followers have negative attitudes which curtail effective mentorship, and the mentor should identify these barriers and address them to maintain a positive mentee-mentor relationship. This requires investing resources in fostering relationships in pursuit of organisational success.

Mentoring in pre-colonial Africa was largely from elders to younger members of society. Among the Tiriki of western Kenya, "it was accepted that knowledge was held almost exclusively by the old; and whether relating to ethics, customs or practical skills, it was passed down largely through participation and observation" (Amatsimbi, 1993, p. 45). Though changing respect for elders is still important in African society where older members of society are acknowledged and consulted when major decisions are made; thus, an older person may be more accepted as a mentor than a younger one. Mentoring includes empowerment which we consider next.

The concept of coaching is closely related to that of mentoring. Mentoring is essentially development driven and considers the whole person. Coaching is usually performance driven and focuses on improvement in specific job-related areas.

Empowerment

Empowerment is granting the power, right or authority to make decisions and perform various duties. It facilitates employees achieving organisational and/or personal goals. It is more than delegation as it includes equipping followers with skills, values and attitudes, and providing resources needed to achieve goals, given their abilities. It requires delegation including guidance, training, time and resources. Empowerment includes tolerance of some mistakes, encouraging experimentation, and allowing followers to treat mistakes as learning opportunities. Some literature suggests innovations are most likely when permission is given to experiment, and when it is easy to be forgiven for trying and failing. Part of empowerment is providing training and coaching, so employees are confident experimenting, and accepting and executing new tasks

High leverage activities are those that benefit both the leader and team most; and Covey says "Once you have a clear picture of your priorities—that is values, goals, and high leverage activities—organize around them" (https://www.pinterest.com/pin/733946668907678055/). Empowering followers frees the leader to concentrate on high-leverage activities rather than day-to-day operations. Once the leader identifies high leverage activities, the leader should have "fire in the belly" as Dr. Manu Chandaria, a Kenyan Industrialist describes the passion to pursue goals to success.

There are many leadership theories and aspects of behaviour that help us understand what constitutes effective leadership. Underlying all of these are questions of trust, justice and ethics, and we look briefly at these in the following discussion.

Trust, Justice and Ethics

Leaders succeed if they are perceived as trustworthy, just and ethical:

- Trustworthiness means being dependable and honest. Bennis (1989) identifies four qualities – constancy, congruity, reliability, integrity and says trust must be earned.
- Justice is concerned with equity and fair treatment. Perceptions of injustice can impair performance. Justice can be seen in how rewards are distributed, how employees are appraised, and how development opportunities are allocated. In the African context, there are traditional justice systems based on oral traditions referred to as 'living customary law' (United Nations Human Rights, 2016).
- Ethics are moral principles governing behaviour and what is right or wrong from a societal/cultural perspective. Values vary across societies affecting right/wrong; thus, leaders need to appreciate different value systems and moral standards. Nevertheless, some ethical principles apply to all leaders, including, honour, integrity, fairness, conscience, responsibility and being principled.

These standards are seen across organisations; for example, in staffing, discrimination based on religion, ethnicity, gender, etc., should be avoided, in buying/selling, trade in counterfeit goods is unethical, in production, environmental pollution should be minimised, in compensation, fair pay is required and so on. Ethical considerations are affected by the laws/regulations of jurisdictions/countries; however, something may be legal but considered unethical in a society and should be avoided. From an organisational perspective, policies should be formulated as guides on trust, justice and ethics as these are attributes that attract the best followers and earn their respect, influencing them to emulate these leaders. An authentic leader who 'walks the talk' and lives by what s/he says will be trusted to explain situations and guide others. Honesty and humility endear leaders to followers, so they can admit mistakes; apologising when something goes wrong does not mean one is less a leader.

We next discuss power, politics and influence in the context of leadership.

Power

Power is the ability to influence others to behave in certain ways, even sometimes against their will. Leadership is a process of influence thus power is inherent in leadership. Power should be used to influence followers to act in ways they embrace and enable them to carry out activities enthusiastically and competently and pursue goals that benefit the organisation. Power is instrumental, enabling the leader to get desired results from those influenced.

The main sources/bases of power are:

Legitimate – power because of position accepted in the social structure. In a community an individual chosen as the chief (traditional chiefs in Ghana and the *Nchuri Ncheke* leaders/elders among the Meru community, and *musakhulu wi idumi*, the ritual elder or custodian of customs, among the Tiriki/vadiriji of in Kenya) has legitimate/position power. They play roles that ordinary community members cannot. In organisations, the structure and hierarchy mean certain decisions are made at particular levels; this avoids conflicts and ensures orderly operations. People occupying certain positions, accepted within the organisational structure, have the right to exercise power commensurate with the position.

Expert – power by virtue of expertise; a professor has power over students because s/he is trained in the subject and can influence students' performance. In organisations, people appointed to positions of power should be those with relevant education, skills and experience, as followers may not respect them if their knowledge seems deficient.

Referent – power related to likeability; someone liked for their eloquence, demeanour, grooming, personality, sense of humour and other attractive attributes. People with strong social convictions also have referent power (for example Mother Teresa of Calcutta). These are often found among socialites and politicians.

Reward – power from the ability to give rewards; at work, this power is exercised by supervisors. People expect rewards for their efforts and a supervisor with this power will influence followers' performance because satisfactory performance is instrumental to accessing rewards.

Coercive – power from sanctions, by inflicting pain; at work, supervisors can refuse requests, dock pay and so on, and may sometimes get compliance through bullying/harassment. The threat or infliction of physical/psychological pain gives power, but it should be applied only if it can bring deviant employees back on track.

Networks/Information – social relationships can be a source of important information and insights, including the acquisition of resources necessary to exert influence on others. A person with valuable networks can influence others who do not have such networks. Being at the centre of a network provides opportunities and thus power.

Boulding (1989) defines power as the ability to get what one wants and lists three categories based on the consequences:

Destructive – includes threats (a manager says "I will fire you if...") and is like coercive power.

Productive – makes and creates positive outcomes (a leader clarifies goals and rewards followers for delivering desired outcomes) and is like reward power.

Integrative – creates relationships and brings people together (a leader appeals to followers and maintains loyalty) and is like referent power.

Boulding (1989) cautions that each type of power has positive and negative uses (a threat may be necessary at certain times), and one type of power may be dominant in some leaders or organisations, but generally there are elements of all present. A leader needs to know which type should be emphasised, depending on the situation – a threat (coercive power) when there is general laxity and 'productive power' when performance targets are accepted by the team. While power is used to influence followers, politics is the process by which power is acquired and retained.

Politics

We often think of politics as the process of gaining state power, sometimes irrespective of the means. Governmental politics has been described as 'a dirty game' where 'the ends justify the means'. Typically, in the quest for political power, contestants will 'cry foul' when they lose but when they 'win' through corrupt practices they do not admit this. In organisations, power can also be gained through 'politicking' and organisational politics are about creating coalitions and support to achieve a particular agenda/interest (sometimes negatively for self-ish interests). To get the attention of a decision maker(s) a subordinate can 'show up' at the right time to be noticed – s/he might pass by the CEO's office to announce, 'I'm working on an innovative process to improve performance', providing an opportunity to talk about other issues, and ensuring they are recognised and remembered later. Such interpersonal relations are a powerful means of gaining organisational power, as is having information that others do not have. Organisational politics are often viewed negatively; however, this is not necessarily the case. Some reasons for organisational politics are:

Access to scarce resources. Leaders/managers establish relation-ships with other managers to get support for their units' plans. Organisations are essentially made up of competing interests and scarce resources are not allocated entirely rationally. The most politically agile managers/employees are more likely to get access to scarce resources.

Promotions. Some employees can sway promotion decisions and rise faster in an organisation, due to politicking. Leaders/man-agers need to be conscious of such activities to avoid the possi-bility of such employees rising to a level of incompetence to the detriment of the organisation.

Teamwork. Teamwork is emphasised in organisations and a manager who can lead a team may need to be politically competent to inter-vene within social networks, win the support of co-workers and erode resistance from others. S/he builds support and advocates for the team's objectives, convincing others to join the team's cause.

In essence, politics can be thought of as influencing others and thus helping to achieve objectives. In this sense, politics in organisations is not negative, although the term has negative connotations.

Influence

Influencing others often relies on the instrumental perspective of power; however, people can also be influenced by the affective per-spective of power, comprising emotions, moods and reflexes. For example, a movie can make people cry, laugh, get angry and so on.

The characters in the movie impacts the audience, elicits emotions and changes moods. The movie influences through its affect. Power is also a two-way interaction, and those with influence can be influenced by their targets. A choir conductor impacts performers through movements, gestures and the baton, and the performers respond and produce the desired effect, in turn animating the conductor. Considering influence as reciprocal helps us better appreciate the dynamics of power and influence in an organisational setting. Leaders should expect to be influenced by the target of their power and need to be sensitive to the use of power and open to the consequences of its exercise. Power then is the ability to influence others and to be influenced by those that we influence.

Culture and Leadership in Africa

Leadership has recently received attention in the African context (Van Zyl et al., 2016), particularly in terms of *Ubuntu*, where community/group needs are considered before the individual's. The leader is expected to stimulate and maintain a spirit of togetherness so that no one falls behind. Leadership comes from a commitment to everyone's improvement. The leader is visionary, wise and a problem solver. Mbigi (2005) described the key values of African leadership as respect/dignity for others, group solidarity and teamwork, service to others and interdependence. This is echoed in the concept that members of a community must bend to the same level to enter a discussion under the 'tree of talking'.

Based on a review of cultural studies that included African countries, Punnett et al. (2019) concluded that there were opposing views of culture and its impact on leadership in the African context. Some writers advocated traditional leadership approaches, others adoption of Western models, and others a hybrid of traditional and Western. Overall, it seems that adherence to humanistic and collaborative values remains important in most African countries, while transformational, visionary and charismatic characteristics are also seen as positive.

The LEAD project focused on African countries. The results showed both personal attributes and behavioural aspects of effective leaders. The following summarises some findings (Melyoki et al., 2018):

> **Personal attributes** – common to Nigeria, Egypt, Kenya and Ghana were *education/being well-educated, visionary, intelligent, team player* (Nigeria), *humility, selflessness* (Ghana), *charisma, competence, good communication* (Ghana), *results oriented, influential* (Kenya) *and* honesty, *integrity* (Uganda).

Important behaviours – Nigeria: *honesty, perseverance, humour, being trustworthy, fair/impartial, results oriented, setting a good example;* Ghana: *respectful, proactive, building a team spirit, setting standards, gives hope, inspires, motivates, 'walks the talk', vision, articulates/communicates goals/vision, rewards performance, leads by example, provides solutions/resources;* Kenya: *goal oriented, achieves team objectives, vision, articulates/ communicates goals/vision, provides solutions/resources and planning/prioritising;* Egypt: *fair, understanding, honest, having commitment and dedication;* Uganda: *inspire, influence.*

These suggest agreement regarding an effective leader in Africa with themes of charisma/transformation, engagement, task, people and so on. LEAD also suggested that spirituality was an important descriptor of effective leaders in the African context.

Conclusion

This overview of leadership draws largely on Western literature from the twentieth century, and it is important to ask whether and how theories apply elsewhere. Much of this discussion is hypothetical, because there is relatively little empirical information available on effective leadership in non-Western societies. A variety of values, attitudes and behaviours are closely connected to effective leadership, including trust, justice, ethics, power, politics, mentoring and empowerment. Culture provides the context in which leadership takes place and understanding cultural issues in Africa can help determine what leadership will be most effective. The LEAD project provides some guidance in this regard. The Western theories discussed in this chapter likely have lessons for leadership in African countries but need to be adapted to the cultural context of these countries.

Review/Discussion

1 Describe three theories of leadership.
2 Compare and contrast the instrumental and affective perspectives to leadership.
3 Discuss how employees can be effectively mentored and empowered in a typical organisation in your country.
4 Discuss the place of religion and spirituality in the effectiveness of leadership in your country.

5 Explain how role theory can improve leadership in organisations in your country.
6 Discuss opportunities for research on power, politics and influence from an organisational perspective.
7 Discuss the motivations for trust, justice and ethics (and lack thereof) for leaders in African countries.

Exercise: Understanding Leadership Through Nelson Rolihlahla Mandela

Thanks to Dr. Theresa A. Chika-James and Brendon Black (MacEwan University).

Leadership has been identified as a fundamental issue impeding the development of African economies. Issues of inadequate infrastructure, problems with democracy, slow uptake in technology and innovation have been attributed to poor leadership. There are many reports of poor leadership and its implications for the economy and citizens, but there are also examples of exemplary leadership in Africa. The case of the legend, President Nelson Rolihlahla Mandela and the end of apartheid in South Africa is a case in point.

Mr. Mandela was a lawyer, a black political activist and a civil rights advocate who significantly contributed to equality, justice and freedom of South Africans. He dedicated his life to fight for social justice and racial equality, and demonstrated exemplary leadership in protests, campaigns, speeches and peaceful negotiations towards the recognition and acceptance of human rights. During his years of protesting against the mistreatment of black South Africans, South African society was described as the great racial divide – a disparity between British and European Colonialists, and Black South Africans, that classified people based on the colour of their skin. Whites were perceived as more civilised and took over more desirable lands. Non-whites were seen as uneducated/uncivil, and forcibly removed from desirable rural areas to live in homelands with rundown huts. More funds towards education were given to white schools and less to black ones, basic education was mandatory for whites from age 7 to 16, and black children from 7 to 13, consequently, black children had fewer employment opportunities or access to further education. In business, black South Africans were perceived by whites as natural resources to be used to transform the rural economy to an industrialised one. Blacks could not establish business in white urban areas/zones, they were prohibited from entering urban areas unless they had jobs there.

Tired of the dehumanisation, Mr. Mandela joined a civil rights activist group, the African National Congress (ANC), and led fellow black South Africans to stage non-violent protests racism. They were faced with police brutality, and were beaten and killed. In the 1960s, Mr. Mandela helped to coordinate a paramilitary group that embraced armed resistance to white police and state brutality. He opted to use violence because non-violence was ineffective. He was resolute in his intention to end the discrimination; however, his pursuit for equality and justice led to his arrest and life imprisonment by the apartheid government in 1963.

In prison, Mr. Mandela was confined to a small cell with no plumbing or bed, and forced to do hard labour in the island quarries. He was permitted to write and receive letters once every six months, and allowed to receive a visitor for 30 minutes once in a year. He wrote letters to his family, other ANC members, and lawyers. Although, he was permitted to write once in every six months, he often had to smuggle the letters to recipients because most of them were confiscated. His writings demonstrated care and love towards his family, the real conditions of prison labour for black prisoners, and his determination to end the apartheid. One smuggled message to ANC members stated:

Unite! Mobilise! Fight on! Between the anvil of united mass action and the hammer of the armed struggle we shall crush apartheid!

Despite harsh prison conditions, his resolve to end social injustice motivated his supporters to continue with local protests. These led to international protests and sanctions against the apartheid government. International and local pressure forced the end of the regime in the early 1990s and Mr. Nelson Rolihlahla Mandela was released from prison, after serving for 27 years. He later became the first democratic President of South Africa on May 10, 1994.

Assignment

1 Based on this description, explain Mr. Mandela's key leadership traits.
2 Discuss Mr. Mandela's leadership competencies.
3 Discuss Mr. Mandela's likely leadership style and why it is effective or ineffective.

References

Amatsimbi, H. M. (1993). *Economic transformation in rural Kenya: A case Study of Tiriki Division, 1902–1963.* A thesis submitted in partial fulfillment for the degree of Master of Arts. University of Nairobi.

Bennis, W. G. (1989). *On becoming a leader.* Reading, MA: Addison-Wesley Pub. Co., Retrieved April 17, 2021, from http://era.gov.kh/eraasset/uploads/2020/02/On-Becoming-a-Leader_BOOK-SUMMARY.pdf

Boulding, K. E. (1989). *Three faces of power.* Newbury Park, CA: Sage Publications. Retrieved April 18, 2021, from https://www.beyondintractability.org/bksum/boulding-three.

Covey, S. R. (2004). *The 7 habits of highly effective people: Restoring the character ethic.* Free Press.

Fiedler, F. E. (1964). "A contingency model of leadership effectiveness". *Advances in Experimental Social Psychology, 1*, 149–190.

House, R. J., & Dessler, G. (1974). The path-goal theory of leadership. Some post hoc and a priori tests. In J. J. Hunt & L. L. Larson (Eds.), *Contingency approaches to leadership* (pp. 29–62). Carbondale, IL: Southern Illinois University Press.

House, R. J., Hanges, P. J., Javidan, M. (2004). *Culture, leadership, and organizations: The Globe Study of 62 societies.* United Kingdom: Sage Publications.

Marques, J. (2020). Inclusive leadership, diversity and wakefulness. In J. Marques (Ed.), *The Routledge companion to inclusive leadership* (pp. 3–12). New York and London: Routledge.

Mbigi, L. (2005). *Ubuntu: The spirit of African transformation management.* Randburg: Knowledge Resources.

Melyoki, L. L., Mukanzi, C. M., Lituchy, T. R., Punnett, B. J., Galperin, B. L., Senaji, T. A. … Osei-Bonsu, N. (2018). Engaged leadership: Lessons from LEAD countries. In Marques, J. & Dhirman, S. (Eds.), *Engaged leadership: Transforming through future oriented design thinking*, Springer International Publishing.

Punnett, B. J., Galperin, B., Lituchy, T., Melyoki, L., Michaud, J., & Mukansi, C. (2019). Cultural values and management in African countries. In C. Simms & B. Hall (Eds.), *Cultures of the World* (pp. 39–100). New York, NY: Nova Publications.

Senaji, T. A., Knight, N. S., Melyoki, L. L., Galperin, B. L., Lituchy, T. R., & Punnett, B. J. (2020). Am I included? Lessons from leadership research in Africa and the African diaspora. In J. Marques (Ed.), *The Routledge companion to inclusive leadership* (pp. 333–345). New York and London: Routledge.

United Nations Human Rights (2016). *Human rights and traditional justice systems in Africa.* New York and Geneva: United Nations Publication. Retrieved April 17, 2021, from https://www.ohchr.org/Documents/Publications/HR_PUB_16_2_HR_and_Traditional_Justice_Systems_in_Africa.pdf

Van Zyl, E., Dalgleish, C., du Plessis, M., Lues, L., Pietersen, E., Ngunjiri, F., & Kablan, P. (2016). *Leadership in the African context.* Cape Town: JUTA.

8 Conflict and Negotiation

Learning Outcomes

After completing this chapter, you will be able to:

- Define and describe conflict and its process
- Explain conflict theories and their applications
- Understand bargaining and negotiation theories
- Describe individual differences in conflict and negotiation situations
- Understand cultural issues in conflict and negotiation in the African context

Thought Starter

The COVID-19 pandemic has clearly illustrated how scarce resources lead to conflicts among people, groups and nations, and the importance of negotiation to ensure a fair distribution of these scarce resources – but who decides what is fair? Throughout the pandemic the World Health Organization has continually called for rich countries to ensure a fair distribution of vaccines, but African countries often found they received a few vaccines while rich countries had high vaccination rates, even for young children, and access to booster shots.

Summary

In this chapter, we define conflict, describe its process and explain conflict theories and their applications. This is followed by bargaining and negotiation and a discussion of individual differences in conflict and negotiation situations. Pertinent Africa context cultural issues are also discussed.

DOI· 10.4324/9781003036838-8

Introduction

When resources are scarce in organisations, individuals and groups compete for them; those who succeed in accessing them are effective negotiators. Inevitably, conflicts arise when there is competition for limited resources. Resources can be anything of value – financial resources, benefits, promotions, attention from top management (including the board of directors) and so on. For example, managers develop strategies and plans for their respective units which are presented to senior management for approvals and allocation of resources to execute them. Those managers who are allocated the most resources are those who present the best plans and successfully negotiate with peers and superiors, while resolving conflicts about their quest for scarce resources.

Conflicts arise within organisations, between organisations and with stakeholders (regulators, customers, creditors, suppliers, debtors, civil society, shareholders, the community). Negotiations are needed to resolve these conflicts, and organisation members who negotiate and achieve desirable results, particularly win-win outcomes, will be rewarded, thus, negotiation skills are important in organisations.

Two major theories that explain conflict are (Folarin, n.d.):

Structural – conflict is a product of tension caused by competition for scarce resources and is inherent in society because of differences in power. Conflict arises due to the nature of human society where some groups dominate others. In organisations, we often think of conflict between management and workers (perhaps represented by a union) which requires engagement and negotiations between management and the workers/union to resolve conflicts and reach positive outcomes.

Marxist – society is divided into unequal classes – one strong and rich (the bourgeoisie who control the instruments of state), the second deprived and socially and financially weak (the proletariat). Hayes (2020) says "conflict theory focuses on competition between groups within society over limited resources ... and views social and economic institutions as tools of the struggle between groups or classes, used to maintain inequality and the dominance of the ruling class" (https://www.investopedia.com/terms/c/conflict-theory.asp).

Both of these, essentially incorporate the idea that conflict arises because resources are scarce and different groups seek control over a greater share of these resources. Of course, we have conflict when it is not so obviously over scarce resources. For example, when people disagree over what television programme to watch or which restaurant to patronise. We also have conflict within ourselves.

Types of Conflict

More broadly, any disagreement or hostility between two or more people can be termed conflict; ranging from extreme religious perspectives of right and wrong to minor arguments over what kind of coffee to stock. Various types of conflict exist and are explained by different disciplines: intrapersonal conflict is rooted in psychology, interpersonal, intra/ intergroup and intraunit conflict in Sociology, while interethnic, interstate and international conflict are based in history and political science.

Groups/teams are emphasised in organisations today and if there are disagreements among team members or between teams they will not perform well and goal achievement will not be realised. Understanding the reasons for conflict is therefore very important for management. Conflict needs to be recognised early on and steps taken to identify the causes and ensure that they are addressed.

Intrapersonal conflict is within a person. Simple intrapersonal conflict might occur if you want to have a second piece of cake and you are worried about putting on weight. More complex issues result in internal psychosomatic disharmony and can include anger, confusion, depression, frustration, aggression, erratic behaviour, addiction and in extreme cases suicide (Ross, 1993). This occurs when a person is torn by different desires/goals and cannot rest because of their unreconciled mental state. This situation can adversely affect their organisational performance if not assessed and dealt with. Some intrapersonal conflict can be dealt with through individual guidance and emotional support, but more extreme cases require outside medical/psychological intervention.

Interpersonal conflict is between/among people and can be caused by many differences, including personality, beliefs, culture, conflicting objectives and so on. Interpersonal conflict may be extreme including direct opposition and violence, or more moderate such as refusing to co-operate or ignoring the 'other side'. Interpersonal conflict can result in individuals not wanting to work together, harassment and in extreme cases, violence. At the individual level, this conflict can be addressed through a conscious realisation that individuals are diverse in many ways and differences need to be acknowledged and accepted. When roles are not clear and members are unsure of who is expected to do what, there are likely to be clashes. Organisational policies play an important part in preventing such conflicts by ensuring role clarity and fairly allocating resources, rewards and sanctions. Management needs to be aware of this kind of conflict to intervene early, and find solutions before the conflict becomes serious.

Intraunit conflict occurs between units in a department or organisation. These conflicts are predominantly about resources and budgetary allocations. For example, the marketing unit may disagree with the finance department over a product promotion budget. Marketing wants to increase promotion and finance wants to limit spending. These conflicts can be resolved through the rational allocation of resources with clear explanations of how these decisions are made. In addition, consensus building regarding organisational priorities helps avoid such disagreements.

Other types of conflict can be with society because organisational policies are at variance with societal norms, with nature if organisational practices degrade the environment, with family where home affects work performance and vice versa.

Some important causes of conflict:

> *Role conflict* – work responsibilities and accountability are unclear, with overlaps in job requirements or status incongruities.
>
> *Personality conflict* – people disagree due to incompatibilities in personalities, approaches to work/life or lifestyle.
>
> Functional conflict – when two or more parties (such as departments in an organisation) with perceived incompatible goals, either consciously or otherwise undermine each other's goal-seeking capability.
>
> *Cultural differences* – people differ based on beliefs, religion, norms and so on.

In Africa, some conflict appears at the community level for political reasons, or over scarce resources such as water or land. There are also perceptions of decisions in appointments as being based on ethnicity/tribe/clan.

Conflict Resolution

In organisations, conflicts usually arise from ambiguous/overlapping roles, perceived unfair distribution of resources, inequity/unfairness, personality and goal conflicts. Resolving such conflicts requires:

* clarity of roles,
* candid and open communication,
* promotion of a culture of trust.

In addition, the dialectic method uses structured dialogue or debate of opposing viewpoints prior to making a decision.

Effective leadership is critical to achieving harmonious relationships among organisational members; a leader who is honest, trustworthy, just and ethical will help followers solve conflicts. These leaders are trusted to facilitate negotiations leading to resolution, or to mediate where necessary. Effective organisational design and staffing, clear job descriptions and specification of functions helps avoid conflicts. When conflicts do arise, communication and interpersonal skills are needed to negotiate a resolution. Further, where a complex conflict is to be resolved, it is desirable to have a 'devil's advocate' who should always give opposing viewpoints for consideration by the conflicting parties. This aids in effective conflict resolution.

Negotiation

In everyday social and organisational encounters conflicts arise and we need to negotiate to resolve them. This may be simple, deciding where to have lunch with colleagues, when one person likes an expensive restaurant and another wants to spend as little as possible, or more complex, negotiating a promotion or salary increase. Socially, it might be negotiating a dowry, common in many African countries or persuading a partner to purchase a new refrigerator.

There are essentially two types of negotiation, *distributive* – where each party aims to maximise gains and the outcome is win-lose/lose-win; and *integrative* – where parties aim to maintain long-term relations through an outcome satisfactory to both, a win-win solution/outcome. Druckman (2007, p. 83) says "many models represent the mixed-motive feature of negotiation where parties are torn between cooperating to get an agreement and competing to get an acceptable agreement close to their own preferences".

Negotiation Process

Negotiation may be defined as a method to arrive at agreement through compromise and to settle differences. The process of negotiation is depicted in Figure 8.1.

The negotiation process has five stages:

Preparation and planning – parties identify issues, interests, possible and desired outcomes, and the negotiation participants.

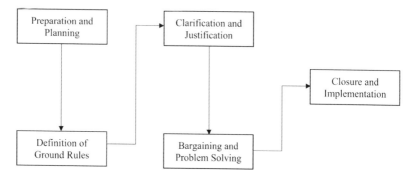

Figure 8.1 Negotiation Process.

Definition and ground rules – parties exchange information and agree on how the negotiation will be conducted, including procedures and norms.

Clarification and justification – parties discuss and clarify their positions, justifying them with relevant facts.

Bargaining and problem solving – this goes back and forth, including 'give-and-take' and compromises.

Closure and implementation – parties reach agreement/disagreement on the issues and proceed to implement outcomes.

Preparation and thought need to be expended to avoid the pitfalls that can lead to failure of negotiations. These include personality differences, impatience, unrealistic expectations or bad faith, where parties pursue selfish interests rather than focusing on win-win solutions.

Personality – as in many other situations personality differences have an impact on negotiations. A very aggressive negotiator may offend others and lead to an early end to negotiations, a very passive one may be too willing to agree with the other side and so on. Negotiators should therefore be selected carefully.

Patience – is said to be a virtue and where stakes are high, patience is indeed a virtue, but keeping expected outcomes in mind should be ensured. A good negotiator lets others speak and disagrees respectfully, giving reasons.

Unrealistic expectations – are a source of negotiations breaking down because if expectations are too high there is no room for concessions to reach agreement and closure.

Bad faith – is problematic because the negotiator is not really interested in reaching agreement, but more interested in getting something for her/himself. For example, instead of focusing on negotiating a partnership agreement (issue), they are concerned with what position they will occupy (selfish interest) in the partnership.

Agreements arise out of bargaining, a common practice in African communities, taking place in daily activities such as purchasing items on the street and in shops, when prices are not fixed. Bargaining consists of the buyer(s) and seller(s) debating the price and merits of the item to be purchased/sold. In Figure 8.1, bargaining/problem solving is the fourth step which precedes closure and implementation. It is an accepted way to exchange goods/services. Bargaining skills should be developed to enable effective navigation through most of the African societies' social, economic and political situations where many issues are negotiated. It is important to develop bargaining skills to avoid unnecessary conflict and achieve the best outcomes; including, the ability to know the worth of a good/service and to see its positives and negatives, to make an informed decision. Someone with good bargaining skills:

- sets realistic expectations,
- anticipates reactions of the other party,
- makes reasonable compromises,
- is assertive but appreciates the other party's position,
- does not settle for a bad outcome,
- knows when to stop negotiating.

In a competitive world we often get what we negotiate, rather than what we deserve; therefore, negotiating skills are important in all aspects of our lives. Developing negotiation skills is relevant for individuals, organisations and society. Individual negotiators approach negotiations with different styles.

Individual Differences

Individual differences have implications for outcomes. Generally, assertiveness has been found to be helpful, particularly when stakes are high. The negotiator should clearly articulate the issues, her/his position, while appreciating the position of the other party.

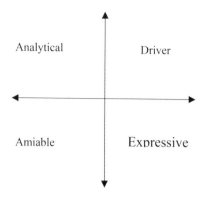

Figure 8.2 Negotiator Personalities.

Some literature indicates four negotiator personalities (see Figure 8.2):

Driver – goal oriented, aims to see results, quick reaction time, decisive, independent, practical, direct, exhibits controlled facial expressions during negotiations.

Expressive – concerned with ideas, the bigger picture, sociable, enthusiastic, impulsive, future oriented, conceptual, innovative, egotistical with a need to be accepted by others; may be undisciplined and easily give concessions.

Amiable – concerned about personal security and acceptance, cooperative, personable, enthusiastic, dislikes conflict and prefers to work in teams.

Analytical – concerned with process, fact oriented, seeking accuracy, organised/systematic, slow in reaction time; they are serious, industrious, tenacious and may too detailed, slowing progress. These four types are also respectively referred to as action, idea, people and process.

The relatively collective nature of African society suggests the amiable personality can facilitate a win-win outcome. Amiables should be complemented with an analytical personality, and an expressive to add some light moments/humour. Drivers'keep negotiations on course, while amiables resolve conflicts and pacify others, and analyticals pay attention to details. Personalities in a negotiation should reflect a combination, selected in terms of expected outcomes, what is at stake and the dynamics likely to be encountered. A 'driver' can make a good negotiation leader, focused on action and result oriented, keeping in mind the objectives of the negotiation.

Prerequisites for Negotiation

Negotiations consist of issues, interests, expectations, the best alternative to a negotiated agreement (BATNA) and the zone of possible agreement (ZOPA).

Issues are the desired agreement or cause of conflict, interests are the stakes that will be gained/lost, what a party loses if negotiations fail, expectations are the favourable outcomes a party hopes to achieve. Issues, interests and expectations should be considered during preparation and clearly defined. Before negotiations start, one should develop a clear understanding of what the issues are and what to do if it is not possible to reach an amicable or desired resolution. It should be clear what we cannot yield and what we can. This is referred to the *best alternative to a negotiated agreement* (BATNA). As part of preparation, each party should be clear about expectations and realise they will not get 100% of what they expect. Parties should be ready to give concessions in terms of a *zone of possible agreement* (ZOPA) where a party is willing to accept the outcome if it falls within this specified range. This range comprises the highest expectations and the lowest below which a party will abandon the negotiations. For example, negotiating the sale of a house, a seller may know that $100,000 is possible, and not be willing to go below $80,000, thus the zopa is $80,000–$100,000.

When negotiations fail, two mechanisms to resolve conflict are mediation or arbitration.

> *Mediation* – is a means of resolving conflicts when the parties agree on a neutral party to facilitate the negotiations by acting as a go-between. The mediator engages in 'shuttle diplomacy' where s/he negotiates with each party in turn, taking notes and briefing the other party, until an agreement is reached. S/he points out to the parties why their expectation may not be realistic, and why a closure is of benefit to the parties. Through this process an agreement and closure is achieved.

> *Arbitration* – uses a person whose decision is final, when both direct and mediated negotiates fail. The arbitrator must be acceptable to all parties. The arbitrator is competent in the area of the conflict, listens to arguments and renders a final binding agreement.

The arbitrator has a legal mandate which a mediator does not have. Both have to be individuals of high moral standing and integrity, to earn the confidence of the parties to the conflict.

Negotiation Skills

It is important that the negotiator has the skills to achieve the best outcomes and there is a premium on effective negotiation skills. These skills do not occur by chance but can be developed through training:

Interpersonal – social skills of relating well with others, explaining one's position clearly and respectfully, exercising an even temperament, and having a sense of humour.

Listening – the ability to listen attentively, politely seek clarification if something is unclear, not interrupt unnecessarily, and acknowledge the other party with courtesy.

Speaking – using the appropriate intonation so you do not appear to be shouting or delivering a lecture, being well composed, articulate and using appropriate body language, showing a sense of tolerance and disagreeing respectfully when presenting counter arguments.

This does not mean that that an effective negotiator is unassertive. Being assertive is always important even as negotiators display decorum and respect. Emotional intelligence is a crucial component of effective negotiations. The effective negotiator needs to know her/his strengths and weaknesses, to be self-aware and know his/her limitations and strengths. From a social/interpersonal perspective, they need to be sensitive to social cues and adjust to these to support progress towards a successful outcome.

Negotiating in good faith means the parties are honest, articulate issues clearly, identify areas of conflict honestly and aim to reach a mutually beneficial agreement. Each party should understand and consider the other party's point of view and maintain respect for this. Disregard for the other party indicates disinterest, and unwillingness to engage in constructive discussions. Negotiating in good faith can result in positive outcomes while negotiating in bad faith will inevitably lead to the collapse of negotiations and the inability to reach an outcome.

One should not go into a negotiation to waste the other party's time. Unnecessarily seeking time off 'to consult principals' can waste time. The negotiator should have the mandate to negotiate and only refer to the principals with full details for final decisions. Though it is common to ask for time off to consult, it is expected that the consultations should be done among the negotiation team rather than taking breaks to go back to principals to get further instructions.

There are also pitfalls to avoid:

Focus on the less important – do not allow smaller details to derail negotiations.

Showing emotions – emotions cloud rational judgment and should be used carefully; if tactics like bluffing, lying and making threats are used they can have negative repercussions.

Not being realistic – do not set expectations too high.

Trying for perfection – accept a good deal and do not try for more which may lead to failure.

Unaware of limits – know the minimum outcome you can accept and be ready to leave if it is not possible.

Not stating what you want – let the other side know what you want and need.

Talking too much, lacking patience not listening – both sides need to be heard, so listen.

Not negotiating in person – a good negotiator uses emotions, body language, heritage and so on, and this is best done in person.

Finally, a good negotiator remains calm, even if negotiations become argumentative – it is better take a 'time-out' rather than to get angry, assess the situation, then come back to the negotiating table, rather than calling off negotiations too quickly. If the other party walks away, however, you should consider whether to end negotiations. Discomfort while negotiating is normal, even for skilled and experienced negotiators, recognition and suppression of frustrations are the hallmark of a skilled negotiator. Of course, a skilled negotiator sometimes uses tactics which appear to be emotional but these are controlled and used intentionally.

Negotiation Outcomes

Outcomes of negotiations are generally classified as win-win, win-lose/lose-win and lose-lose. Win-win is an outcome where all parties are satisfied with the outcome, while lose-lose is where all parties are dissatisfied, win-lose/lose-win implies that one party is satisfied (wins) and the other not (loses). A win-win outcome is desirable because the relationship between the parties is likely to continue after the negotiation, and both parties are likely to work to achieve mutually desirable objectives. A win-lose outcome may seem beneficial to the winning party, but the losing one will look for opportunities to settle scores in future and will not work towards objectives. Lose-lose outcomes are those where negotiations break down, no agreement is reached, and these are not desirable for either party.

Cultural Issues

Adler (1991) proposed that all negotiations consist of four stages – relationship building, exchange of task-related information, persuasion and making concessions and reaching agreement. She argued that the sequence and timing of these stages varied based on cultural preferences. Some cultures see building relationships as a pre-requisite to doing business and spend a lot of time on this stage, others focus on relationships only after reaching an agreement. Some cultures are detailed and specific in terms of task-related information, others prefer to be general and allow for unknowns. Some cultures are aggressive in terms of persuasion, others are lower keyed. Some cultures make concessions throughout negotiations, others all at once at the end. Some require written, detailed, formal agreements, others prefer more informal verbal ones.

The collective culture in Africa suggests that relationship building will be important and that negotiating parties may be relatively comfortable with informal, verbal agreements. The collectivist, high power distance and masculinity nature of most of African societies may have important implications for the nature, type and outcome of negotiations. High collectivism suggests an *integrative* (collaborative) approach seeking a win-win outcome, while masculinity may promote a *distributive* (competitive) negotiation seeking a win-lose outcome. It is not clear which will predominate, but one might expect to encounter either or both in African negotiations. Time orientation is relatively short in Africa and may affect the timeframe for negotiations and the desired outcomes; with negotiations taking place over a relatively short period and focusing on shorter-term goals and objectives. This model is applicable in the Africa setting, with greater emphasis on relationships where substantial effort is expended to ensure that relationships are maintained and amicable solutions realised. In some case there may be a fatalistic tendency of 'leave it to God' or 'God willing'.

Review/Discussion

1 Explain how personality impacts conflict in organisations.
2 Discuss the link between culture and conflict in organisations in Africa.

3 Explain the different methods of conflict resolution.
4 Discuss the various pitfalls in negotiation as a conflict resolution mechanism.
5 Using African cultural characteristics, discuss the stages of negotiation proposed by Adler.

Exercise: Mediation

An example of mediation is Kenya's 2007 presidential election dispute and post-election violence of 2007–2008 that left a trail of death and internal population displacement. Due to the nature of the dispute and the high stakes involved, both parties were persuaded to embrace mediation, and Dr. Kofi Annan (former Secretary General of the United Nation) sent his envoy, President John Kufuor of Ghana, to Kenya for mediation in the conflict between Mwai Kibaki (Party of National Unity) and Raila Odinga (Orange Democratic Movement). The latter's position was that the election had been rigged in favour of the former, who was running for his second and last term and had been hurriedly sworn-in at dusk. This conflict led to violence which resulted in lives lost, displacement of population groups, and other crimes that met the threshold of 'crimes against humanity', resulting in the trial of some Kenyans at the international criminal court at The Hague. Dr. Kofi Annan played an important role in mediating and arriving at the creation of the 'grand coalition government' with Mwai Kibaki as president and Raila Odinga as prime minister. Since the disputed election had resulted in unprecedented violence, the first condition was for the parties to cease violence to pave the way for conflict resolution in a calm environment.

Assignment

1 Discuss why mediation was necessary.
2 Explain what issues to you think arose during the mediation.
3 Identify the characteristics you think the lead mediator had.
4 Identify and discuss the motivations of the conflicting parties for accepting a mediated agreement.

References

Adler, N. J. (1991). *International dimensions of organizational behavior*. Boston, MA: PWS-Kent Publishing.

Druckman, D. (2007). Negotiation models and applications. In Avenhaus R. & Zartman I.W. (Eds.), *Diplomacy games* (pp. 83–96). Berlin, Heidelberg: Springer. DOI:10.1007/978-3-540-68304-9_5

Folarin, S. F. (n.d.). *Chapter three: Types and causes of conflict.* Retrieved February 15, 2022, from http://eprints.covenantuniversity.edu.ng/3241/1/ Folarin%2025.pdf

Hayes, S. C. (2020). *Acceptance and commitment therapy: Principles of becoming more flexible, effective, and fulfilled.* Louisville, CO: Sounds True.

Ross, E. I. (1993). *Write now.* New York, NY: Barnes & Noble Publishing.

Index